Cooking with Honey

The Natural Way
to
Better Eating and Good Health

by

Marge Davenport

with special credits to
National Honey Board
and
Oregon State Beekeepers Association

Paddlewheel Press

Publishers
P.O. Box 230220
Tigard, Oregon 97223

ISBN 0-938274-05-8

Chehalem Printing
© Copyright 1992

$13.95

Editor's Note

Honey is so good, so pure, and can add so much to cooking that I found it surprising that there are few good honey recipes in print. To remedy this—to help you enjoy healthy and delicious honey and honey-made foods, and to give you new ways and ideas about how to use honey in all kinds of dishes, we give you "Cooking with Honey".

Inspired by the Oregon State Beekeepers Association, who are the folks who keep the bees that make some of the finest honey in the world, and encouraged by the National Honey Board, "Cooking with Honey" was made possible. Many of the recipes were tested in their research kitchens.

Special thanks to the many other people who have helped: Lydge Cady, co-publisher, who really should be listed as co-author, but demurred; Majorie Ehry, president of the Oregon State Beekeepers Association, and Joann Olstrom of Joann's Honey, home economist, and a mover in the Beekeepers Association, and to Chehalem Printing, Newberg, Oregon.

I hope "Cooking with Honey" adds 'The Golden Touch' to your cooking and brightens your foods and your life!

Introduction

Two kinds of people get special pleasure from cookbooks: those who are delighted by interesting recipes and who carefully select recipes they want to try. These cooks follow the directions meticulously and carefully measure and blend. To them, discovery of great new recipe adds a new delight to their file of favorites.

Then there are the cookbook collectors — they love cookbooks. Their book shelves are lined with them. they can't resist a new cookbook and they take each new one home and read it cover to cover. But they infrequently follow any one recipe. Instead, they read for inspiration, for new ideas, and they incorporate these into their cooking to make cooking an adventure and delight.

"Cooking with Honey" is a cookbook for all cooks. It opens an almost forgotten and neglected facet of our gastronomical heritage — enjoying and taking advantage of all the benefits and joys of using and cooking with honey.

Earliest civilizations knew, appreciated and reveled in honey. It was an important part of their diet, a special treat, and a part of their medicine chest and their beauty aids.

To the Greeks, honey was the 'nectar of the gods' and was considered 'a gift from heaven.' Assuming the gods could eat whatever they wanted, it seemed logical that they would choose honey, the most delicious food of all.

Honey was also important to the Egyptians, and important in ancient China and India. It is mentioned positively in both the Bible and the Koran. Primitive people also knew the benefits of honey and old cave paintings indicate they sometimes risked their lives to obtain it.

Now, as in former times, honey remains one of the most remarkable foods in the world. Pure and natural, it requires no processing or chemical additives. It will keep indefinitely without refrigeration. It is a preservative, and is easier to digest than processed sugar. Best of all, honey is delicious, either by itself or as a nutritious and subtle flavoring and enhancer in other foods.

Honey, then, is being rediscovered by food lovers everywhere. There is a honey revolution underway. Honey, we're glad you are back.

These recipes in "Cooking with Honey" can add a new dimension to your cooking and to your enjoyment of food and life. Try it and you will agree — a magical substance, honey!

Is honey really a natural product? *All honey is a natural sweet made up of simple sugars, mainly fructose and glucose. The glucose provides energy. Fructose gives honey its unique flavor. Honey also contains traces of minerals, vitamins and enzymes.*

What is the best way to store honey? *In a dry place, as honey absorbs moisture. Refrigeration will hasten granulation. Freezing does not injure honey.*

What should I do with granulated honey? *Granulation is a natural process of true pure honey. All honey will granulate in time but never spoils. Granulation does not affect honey's taste or purity. It may be used granulated or restored to liquid.*

How do I reliquefy honey? *Place container (never plastic) in pan of warm (not hot) water. For microwave: Cook (glass only) on HIGH for 1 to 1-1/2 minutes, uncovered. Let stand 5 minutes. To protect its delicate color and flavor, do not overheat.*

Does honey have additives? *All honey is pure with no additives or preservatives. No sodium.*

How many types of honey are available? *In addition to liquid honey, there is creamed honey (which is finely crystallized). Comb honey is available during certain times of the year. Cut comb is sometimes placed in jars of honey. Remember, the comb is edible.*

Are there less calories in honey? *Although caloric value of honey is slightly higher, the fructose provides more sweetening per measure reducing the amount required and the calories.*

What is the most economical size container to purchase? *The larger the size container, the more economical. For easier handling, pour into smaller containers. Cover tightly. Remember, honey is heavy by weight. A 12 oz jar equals one standard 8 oz measuring cup.*

May other sweeteners be replaced by honey? *Recipes especially created and tested for honey give the best results. In many of your favorite recipes you may replace 1 cup of dry sweetener with 2/3 or 3/4 cup of honey depending on sweetness desired. Oil or wet measuring cup for easy pouring. Reduce baking temperature 25° F.*

Table of Contents

Honey Tips

Cooking Tips:

- *For best results, use recipes that specify honey.*

- *When you substitute honey for granulated sugar in recipes:*

  - *Substitute honey for up to 1/2 the sugar.*

  - *With experimentation, honey can be substituted for all the sugar in some recipes.*

  - *Reduce the amount of liquid in the recipe by 1/4 cup for each cup of honey used.*

  - *In baked goods, add about 1/2 teaspoon baking soda for each cup of honey used.*

  - *Honey adds a golden color to baked goods, to prevent over-browning, reduce oven temperature by 25° F.*

  - *For easy removal, coat measuring cup with vegetable cooking spray before adding honey.*

Honey absorbs and retains moisture readily so baked goods will stay fresh longer.

Honey Spreads like those shown on Page 7 are easy to make, and great to have handy. Store in refrigerator where they keep indefinately. Try Blueberry Spread (Page 34), Honey Butter (10), and Cheese Spread (32), and then experiment.

Storage Tips

- Store at room temperature.

- If honey crystallizes, remove lid and place jar in warm water until crystal dissolves. Or microcook at HIGH (100%) 2 to 3 minutes or until crystal dissolves; stir every 30 seconds. Do not boil or scorch.

Buying Tips

- Select mildly flavored honeys, such as clover, for use in cooking where delicate flavors predominate.

- Use strongly flavored honeys in spreads or other recipes where a distinct honey flavor is desired.

- When possible, buy honey in bulk.

CANDIED ORANGE PEEL

Peel of 3 oranges   1 cup honey

Remove peel from oranges in quarter sections. Boil in salted water until very tender. Drain. Cut into strips. Bring honey to boil. Add orange peel. Cook gently for 10 minutes.

HONEY FRESH FRUIT DIP

1   cup mayonnaise   1/4 cup honey
1/2   cup lemon juice

Combine with container of yogurt or whipped cream. Add nutmeg as a garnish. Now select and wash a variety of fresh fruit such as strawberries, grapes, pineapple, pear, apple and banana — use your imagination. Dip with toothpicks and enjoy.

PEACH FROSTY

1-1/2 cups peach nectar   1 Tbs honey
Juice of 2 lemons   1 egg white

Put crushed ice in blender. Add the other ingredients. Beat until well mixed and frothy. Pour into chilled goblets and serve.

HONEY BUTTER

1/2 cup soft butter   1/2 cup honey

Let butter stand at room temperature until softened. Gradually add an equal amount of honey, beating until the honey is well blended with the butter.

SAVORY BEETS
"Sweet-Sour Flavor"

2 cups diced cooked beets or 1 can   2 Tbs chopped onions
  (16 oz) diced beets, drained   3 Tbs cider or wine vinegar
3 Tbs butter or margarine   1 tsp salt
1 Tbs honey

Cook onion in butter until soft but not brown. Add vinegar.

HONEY ICE CUBES

1/2 cup honey   2 Tbs lemon juice
2 cups very hot water

Blend ingredients and freeze. Good in iced tea or punch.

ORANGE HONEY-ADE

2 cups orange juice   1/2 cup honey
1/2 cup lemon juice   1 cup water

Combine all ingredients in a blender. Blend until honey is dissolved. Pour over cracked ice in tall glass. Garnish with orange slice and cherries. Serves 4.

HONEY GLAZE FOR MEATS AND HAM

Combine 1/2 cup honey, 1/4 cup soy sauce and 1 tsp mustard.

HONEY GINGER CREAM

2 cups whipping cream   1/2 tsp ginger
1/4 cup honey

Whip 2 cups whipping cream until stiff. Gradually add 1/4 cup honey and 1/2 tsp ginger. Chill one hour before serving. Makes 4 cups of topping.

SUMMER SALAD

1 cup watermelon balls   1/4 cup honey
1 cup cantaloupe (or honeydew balls)   Juice of 1 lemon
1/2 cup whipped cream

Cut balls from ball cutter (or cube the fruit). Sprinkle with lemon juice, then honey and chill. Fold whipped cream into fruit just before serving, on crisp lettuce. Serves 4 to 5.

QUICK HONEY FROSTING

8 oz pkg cream cheese   1/4   cup soft honey

Bake a plain white or yellow cake in a 13" x 9" x 2" pan. Cool. Frost with an 8 oz pkg of cream cheese combined with 1/4 cup soft honey. Cream until smooth. Cover top of cake and sprinkle with fine nuts. Refrigerate cake.

QUICKIE SALAD DRESSING

1/2 cup mayonnaise
2 Tbs warmed honey

2 Tbs red wine vinegar
1/8 to 1/4 tsp paprika

Warm honey in microwave for a few seconds (makes mixing easier). Mix all ingredients together in a bowl with a wire whip. Refrigerate.

WHIPPED CREAM
Sweetened With Honey

1/2 cup whipping cream
1/2 tsp vanilla

1 Tbs light honey

Chill beaters and cream. Whip to soft peaks, slowly mix in honey and vanilla. Keep chilled.

Tasty Salads and Vegetables

Have you ever noticed how many items in your store feature honey? There are honey grahams. Honey cereals. Honey sauces. Honey dressings. Honey mustard. Honey nuts. The list goes on and on.

That's because honey adds beautiful golden color and delightful sweet flavor to bring out the best in so many foods.

In just minutes, you can add the magic of honey to your meals. Whip up a sparkling honey vinaigrette dressing for sensational salads. Sauce your meat and chicken with the rich, sweet flavor of a tangy honey blend. For a grand finale, finish with your favorite ice cream, topped with beautiful rivers of flavored honey.

You can add this magic ingredient to many of your favorite dishes. Try these honey ideas for starters.

Enjoy the golden touch.

Marinated Carrots

Marinated Carrots will keep in the refrigerator for up to three weeks, but you may be not able to keep them that long. Serve with salads, as appetizer, or with meals as a tangy relish.

INGREDIENTS:

1	can tomato soup		3/4	cup apple-cider vinegar
1-1/2	tsp hot Tabasco		1	tsp dry mustard or prepared mustard
1/4	cup canola oil		2	lbs cooked carrots (do not overcook)
1/2	cup honey		1	medium onion, sliced
1	medium bell pepper, sliced or slivered raw			

METHOD:

Whip all marinade ingredients well. Drop pepper and onion slices into marinade. Pour marinade over drained, slightly cooked, sliced carrots. Place in refrigerator. Chill for 8 to 12 hours before serving. Will keep up to 3 weeks in refrigerator (if you can keep them, that long).

Honey-Sesame Dressing with Icicle Radish Salad

Variety in salads helps pep up meals. This is a good one to serve guests, or at special family affairs.

INGREDIENTS:

1/2	cup <u>each</u> vegetable oil and rice wine vinegar
1 to 2	Tbs grated ginger root
3/4	tsp sesame oil
	Salt to taste

1/4	cup honey
3	Tbs toasted sesame seeds
1	small clove garlic, minced
1/8	tsp crushed dried red pepper

METHOD:

Combine ingredients; mix thoroughly. Serve with Icicle Radish Salad. Makes 1 1/3 cups dressing.
ICICLE RADISH SALAD: Arrange on serving platter 3 cups fresh spinach, torn into bite-sized pieces, 1 cup <u>each</u> julienne icicle radishes and carrots and 1 cup bean sprouts, optional. Spoon on desired amount of Honey-Sesame Dressing. Makes 4 to 6 servings.

Honey Pear Salad

Makes six servings.

INGREDIENTS:

3	large ripe pears, cored, pared and diced
1-1/2	cups dices celery
1/2	cup seedless raisins
1	Tbs honey
1	Tbs lemon juice
1/3	cup mayonnaise or salad dressing
	Lettuce

METHOD:

Combine pears, celery, and raisins in medium-size bowl. Stir honey and lemon juice into mayonnaise or salad dressing in 1 cup measure; pour over fruit and toss to mix; chill/ Spoon into lettuce cups. Makes 6 servings.

Four Bean Salad

Simple, but good. Honey adds "the golden touch" that makes the dressing special.

INGREDIENTS:

1	can each: red kidney beans, green beans yellow and garbanzo beans	1	large onion cut in thin wedges
1/2	tsp celery seed or chopped fresh celery (1/2 cup)	1	green pepper (chopped)
1/2	cup salad oil	3/4	cup vinegar
		3/4	cup honey (mild)

METHOD:

Heat vinegar, oil and honey, just to blend. Pour over bean mixture. Best if refrigerated at least 3 hours before serving. Keeps well.

Sour Cream for Fruit Salads

A quick dressing that makes fruit salad special.

INGREDIENTS:

1	cup sour cream
1	tsp grated orange rind
1	Tbs orange juice
1	Tbs lemon juice
1	Tbs honey
1/2	tsp dry mustard
1	tsp salt
1-1/4	tsps paprika

METHOD:

Whip the sour cream, combine the remaining ingredients. Fold mixtures together and chill. Keep refrigerated. Makes 1-1/2 cups.

Sweet and Sour Spinach Salad

This salad is better if you pour the dressing over it while it is still hot.

INGREDIENTS:

3	slices bacon
3	Tbs honey
2 to 3	Tbs juice of lemon
2	Tbs grated cheddar
	Bib lettuce, fresh spinach,
	a few fresh mushrooms or bean sprouts.

2 to 3	Tbs tarragon vinegar
2	tsp lemon peel (grated)
1/2	cup chopped apples or pears
1	hard cooked egg (sliced)

METHOD:

Cut bacon in little pieces and fry it crispy. Add all at once: vinegar, honey and lemon juice. Simmer no more than 2 minutes. Mix lettuce, spinach, apple, mushrooms or bean spouts. Pour bacon mixture over salad. Toss lightly. Makes 2 large or 4 small salads. Garnish with grated cheese and egg.

Raw Fresh Applesauce

This is a refreshing treat. Add a 1/2 tsp of powdered ascorbic acid to keep apple color bright.

INGREDIENTS:

3	apples, pared, cored and diced
1/4	cup apple juice, orange or pineapple juice
1/4	cup mild flavored honey

METHOD:

Place all ingredients in blender or food processor. Purèe to desired smoothness.
Makes about 1-1/2 cups.

Honeyed Squash

Danish, Hubbard, or any hard-shelled squash is good in this recipe.

INGREDIENTS:

3	medium acorn squash
1/2	tsp salt
1/4	cup butter
1/4	tsp ginger
1/4	tsp cinnamon
1/3	cup honey

METHOD:

Preheat oven to 375° F. Cut squash in half and clean. Place open side down in 1/2" of hot water, bake 1/2 hour. Pour off water - turn right side up and put butter, honey, seasoning mixture in each. Return to oven and bake 1/2 hour.

Wintery Stir-Fry

A vegetarian treat.

INGREDIENTS:

<u>Prepare Vegetables</u>
1/4   cup onion, cut in slivers
1   cup carrots, sliced in thin "pennies"
1   cup broccoli, thin slices

<u>Heat Skillet</u>: add
1 to 2 tsp oil
1/4   tsp salt
        The vegetables
        Stir-Fry a few minutes

METHOD:

Add 1/4 cup water: cover; steam gently 4 minutes. No water should remain. Add and mix gently: 1 grapefruit, sectioned, or 1 tomato, cut in wedges; 1 to 2 tsps honey dressing. Serve at once. 2 to 4 servings.

Zucchini Twists

This can be a dinner vegetable, or can even serve as a main dish. It's another way to help use 'all that zucchini'.

INGREDIENTS:

2   cups zucchini, quartered and cut into 2 inch pieces
1/2   cup honey
2   cups fresh bread cubes
1/2   tsp paprika (optional)

METHOD:

Layer bottom of baking dish with bread cubes. Place layer of zucchini on top and drizzle honey lightly over top. Repeat layers, topping each with honey. Bake in 350° F. oven for 30 minutes or until zucchini is tender.

Sweet and Sour Zucchini

You can't have too many recipes for zucchini. This can be served as a vegetable or as a salad.

INGREDIENTS:

1-1/2 Tbs chopped onion	1/2 to 3/4 cup mild flavored honey
1 cup white wine vinegar	1/2 cup chopped green pepper
1 tsp pepper	1/3 cup salad oil
1/2 cup diced celery	1 tsp salt
7 small zucchini, thinly sliced	

METHOD:

Combine all ingredients in large bowl. Cover and refrigerate overnight. Drain and serve chilled or at room temperature. Makes about 2 quarts.

Easy Baked Beans

A healthy dish that combines lots of different kinds of beans. Save any leftover—it's great reheated.

INGREDIENTS:

1	can (32 oz) pork and beans		1	can (15-1/2 oz) drained <u>each</u>:
1/2	cup chopped onions			garbazo beans, butter beans, and
1/2	cup bacon or ham			pinto beans
2	cans kidney beans, drained		1/2	cup ketchup
1/2	cup prepared mustard		1	cup (dark) honey
1/2	cup brown sugar		1/2	cup molasses (optional) if a stronger flavor needed

METHOD:

Place all ingredients in 4 quart pan or baking dish and cook on medium for 45 minutes to an hour,. If baking in the oven, bake 1 hour at 350° F.. Stir occasionally, to prevent sticking. If desired, canned pineapple can also be added.

Honey Baked Beans

This is a good dish to take to a potluck. It will disappear fast.

INGREDIENTS:

4	slices bacon, diced
1/2	cup chopped onions
4-1/2	cups cooked navy beans (3 cans, 15 oz each, cooked navy beans can be substituted)
1/2	cup honey
1/2	cup ketchup
1	Tbs <u>each</u> prepared mustard and Worchestershire sauce

METHOD:

Sautè bacon and onion until onion is tender; combine with remaining ingredients in shallow 2 qt oven-safe baking dish. Cover with lid or aluminum foil and bake at 350° F. for 30 minutes. Uncover and bake 45 minutes longer. Makes 4 to 6 servings.

Spreads and Butters

Breakfast Important for Health and Well-Being

Over and over again, we're being told how important breakfast is to our health and well being.

- According to a group of California nutritionists, people who eat breakfast may actually live longer than those of us who, at 6:00 in the morning, are lucky to find time for a shot of caffeine.

- Kelly Brownell, a psychologist at Penn State University, claims eating a good breakfast can also have an effect on your feeling of well-being—the same effect as running several miles, propelling you through the day with a positive attitude.

- Marion Cunningham, author of the "Breakfast Book", says breakfast is more than a meal; it's a feeling that represents comfort and home.

With Americans having little time for anything more extravagant than toast or muffins before rushing off to work, the morning meal can easily become dull and monotonous. Since breakfast is such a healthy, uplifting and comforting meal, it behooves us to make it appealing enough to keep us from skipping it altogether. Pep up your breakfast with these handy spreads.

Honey Pear Butter

INGREDIENTS:

2	qts pear pulp
1	cup light honey
1/3	cup orange juice
	Nutmeg
1	tsp orange rind

METHOD:

Core pears and slice. Cook until soft. Add little water to prevent sticking to pan. Put through sieve. Measure pulp in large pan. Add the rest of ingredients and honey . Cook until thick. Stir to keep from sticking, or cook in crock pot. Pour into hot jars, leaving 1/4" head space. Put on lids and place in boiling water bath for 10 minutes. Makes 4 pints.

Spiced Apple Honey Butter

This butter can be stored in the refrigerator for 2 months, or can be canned or frozen.

INGREDIENTS:

4	Lbs (about 12 medium-size) tart apples		1	cup water
1	qt apple juice		1/4	cup lemon juice
1/2	tsp salt		2	tsps ground cinnamon
1/2	tsp ground cloves		1/4	tsp <u>each</u> ground ginger and nutmeg
1-1/2	cups light, mild-flavored honey			

METHOD:

Quarter and core unpeeled apples. In a 6 qt or larger pan, combine apples, water, apple juice and lemon juice. Cover and simmer over medium-low heat until fruit is soft (about 30 minutes). Using metal blade, process mixture, a portion at a time, until puréed. Return purée to pan. Add salt, cinnamon, cloves, ginger, nutmeg and honey. Cook, uncovered, over low heat for 1 to 1-1/2 hours, stirring frequently as butter thickens. Makes about 3 pints.

TO FREEZE BUTTER: Spoon cooled butter into freezer containers or jars to within 1" of top. Cover

TO CAN BUTTER: Fill sterilized jars, seal and boil in hot water bath (jars covered with water) for 25 minutes.

Honey Blueberry Spread

Keep this spread in the refrigerator and serve with meals or as a between meal snack on special breads.

INGREDIENTS:

1/2   cup fresh or frozen blueberries, thawed
1/4   cup honey, divided
1/2   cup butter or margarine, softened to room temperature

METHOD:

Bring blueberries and 2 Tbs honey to boil over medium-high heat stirring constantly; cook 3 to 4 minutes or until mixture thickens and is reduced by half. Cool. Blend in honey. Beat in butter. makes about 2/3 cup. Preparation Time: About 15 minutes.

Ginger-Pear Honey Butter

Fresh pears and ginger team up with honey for a piquant spread to keep in the refrigerator for a month, or to freeze or can for use all winter.

INGREDIENTS:

4	Lbs (about 8 large) Bartlett pears
1/4	cup lemon juice
1/2	tsp salt
3/4	tsp ground ginger
1-1/2	tsp grated lemon peel
1	cup light, mild-flavored honey

METHOD:

Quarter and core unpeeled pears. In a 6 qt or larger pan, combine pears and lemon juice. Cook, covered, over medium-low heat, stirring occasionally, until fruit is soft (about 30 minutes). Using metal blade, process mixture, a portion at a time, until puréed. Return purèe to pan; add salt, ginger, lemon peel and honey. Cook, uncovered, over low heat for 1-1/2 to 2 hours, stirring more frequently as butter thickens. Makes about 2 pints.

TO CAN BUTTER: Fill hot sterilized jars, seal and boil in hot water bath for 25 minutes.

TO FREEZE BUTTER: Spoon cooled butter into freezer or jars to within 1" of top. Cover and freeze.

Honey Cheese Spread

This versatile spread is equally good with fresh fruit or on specialty breads.

INGREDIENTS:

1	cup ricotta cheese
1/2	cup plain yogurt
3	Tbs honey
1/2	cup whipping cream

METHOD:

In small bowl crumble the ricotta cheese. Add plain yogurt and honey; beat well. Beat cream on medium speed just until soft peaks form: fold into the cheese mixture. Turn mixture into serving bowl or crock (or cover and chill until needed, up to 4 days). Serve with slices of apples, pears, and nut bread. **NOTE:** Dip apple and pear slices in mixture of water and lemon juice or ascorbic acid color keeper to prevent them from discoloring.

Spiced Honey Butter

This will keep for several weeks in the refrigerator. Serve with biscuits, bread or toast.

INGREDIENTS:

1/2	cup butter or margarine, softened to room temperature
1/4	cup honey
1	tsp grated orange peel
1/2	tsp ground cinnamon

METHOD:

Combine all ingredients and mix well. Makes about 3/4 cup. Preparation Time: Less than 15 minutes.

Honey Hazelnut Spread

INGREDIENTS:

1/2   cup honey
1/2   cup butter or margarine
1/2   cup ground, roasted, skinned hazelnuts
      (one tsp brandy flavoring may be substituted)

METHOD:

Roast hazelnuts in flat pan at 325* F. 15 minutes or until skins blister and nuts are lightly colored. Cool slightly; rub between palms of hands or with clean towel to remove skins. Cream honey and butter; stir in hazelnuts. Makes 1 1/4 cups. Preparation Time: About 30 minutes.

Honey Brandy Spread

INGREDIENTS:

1/4   cup butter or margarine, softened
1-1/2 cups creamed honey
2   Tbs brandy (one tsp brandy flavoring can be substituted)
1/8   tsp ground nutmeg

METHOD:

Beat butter until creamy. Stir in honey, 1/2 cup at a time; beat until smooth. Stir in brandy and nutmeg. Refrigerate. Makes 2 1/4 cups. Preparation Time: About 15 minutes.z

Honey Mustard Mayonnaise

Spread on meatloaf, pork loin, ribs or chicken pieces during last 15 minutes of baking or serve as dipping sauce.

INGREDIENTS:

1	cup catsup
1/4	cup honey
1	tsp prepared mustard
1/2	tsp ground nutmeg

METHOD:

Combine all ingredients, mix thoroughly. Makes 1-1/4 cups.

Honey Pecan Sticky Buns

Breads, Muffins, Rolls

Honey was first introduced to America in 1638 when European colonists brought honeybees to the colonies. Referred to as "White Man's Flies" by North American natives, the bees quickly adapted to their new environment and the honey they produced was creatively utilized in food and beverage preparation, fruit preservation, making cement, concocting furniture paste-polish and varnish, and for medicinal purposes.

Now, almost 400 years following their initial arrival on American soil, honeybees produce over 227 million pounds of honey annually in the United States. And, although it's no longer offered to the Gods, fed to sacred animals or used to make cement, honey continues to sweeten our lives and palates with its natural distinctive and unmistakable flavor.

Honey adds a smooth distinctive flavor to an old familiar favorite — Honey Pecan Sticky Buns. (Pictured on page 37 — Recipe on page 39)

Honey Pecan Sticky Buns

These sticky buns will disappear in a hurry!

INGREDIENTS:

1	package (16 oz) hot roll mix
1	cup hot water (120° to 130° F.)
1	egg
1/4	cup packed brown sugar
1	tsp ground cinnamon

6	Tbs sugar, divided
1/2	cup butter or margarine, divided
1/3	cup honey
1/4	cup pecan halves

METHOD:

From package combine flour mix, yeast and 2 Tbs sugar; mix thoroughly. Add water, 2 Tbs butter and egg; stir until dough pulls away from sides of bowl. Turn into lightly floured surface; knead about 5 minutes or until smooth. If needed, sprinkle with additional flour to reduce stickiness. Cover dough; let rest 5 minutes. Heat honey, 4 Tbs butter and brown sugar until melted; stir until thoroughly mixed. Spoon evenly into 13" x 9" x 2" baking pan; sprinkle with pecans. Roll dough to 12" x 10" rectangle; melt remaining 2 Tbs butter and spread over dough. Combine remaining 1/4 cup sugar and cinnamon; sprinkle over dough. Roll up along 12" side; pinch seam to seal. Cut into 12 one inch slices; place in pan cut-side down. Bake at 350° F. 25 to 30 minutes or until lightly browned. Immediately invert onto heat-proof serving plate. Let pan remain 2 to 3 minutes to allow to drizzle over rolls. Makes 12 rolls. Preparation Time: Less than 45 minutes. Bake Time: About 25 to 30 minutes.

Honey White Bread

Once you start baking with honey you will appreciate the way it helps keep your breads and rolls fresh and moist longer.

INGREDIENTS:

2   cups warm water
2   pkgs active yeast
1/2   cup honey
1   tsp salt
1/4   cup shortening
1   egg
6-1/2 to 7 cups flour

METHOD:

In a bowl dissolve yeast in water. Stir in honey, salt, egg and shortening. Mix in enough flour to make dough easy to handle. Cover and let rise 1-1/2 to 2 hours. Knead and place in baking pan and let rise again. Bake at 400° F. for 20 minutes, reduce heat to 350° F. and bake another 20 minutes. Cool on rack.

Honey Nut Bread

Every bit as good as banana bread. Slice Honey Nut Bread thin and enjoy.

INGREDIENTS:

1	cup mild honey		1	cup milk
1/2	cup sugar		1/4	cup butter
2	egg yolks		2-1/2	cups sifted flour
1	tsp baking soda		1	tsp cinnamon
1/2	tsp salt		1	cup hazelnuts

METHOD:

Combine honey, milk, sugar and butter in a saucepan. Heat slowly until sugar dissolves and butter melts. Cool then pour into large bowl. Sift dry ingredients together and carefully fold into honey mixture. Fold in nuts. Butter 2 small loaf pans. Line with wax paper and butter paper. Pour in batter and let stand 15 to 20 minutes. Bake at 350° F. for 40 to 50 minutes. Cool on rack.

Honey Zucchini Bread

Honey helps keep this bread moist and delectable. Use egg whites to lower cholesterol.

INGREDIENTS:

3	eggs (or 4 egg whites and 1 yolk)	1	cup vegetable oil
1	cup honey	3	tsps vanilla extract
2	cups grated zucchini, unpeeled	3	cups all purpose flour
1	tsp soda	1/2	tsp baking powder
1	tsp salt (less for restricted diets)	1	cup finely chopped nuts

METHOD:

Mix beaten eggs, oil, honey, vanilla and zucchini. In another bowl mix flour, baking soda, baking powder and salt. Add egg mixture to dry ingredients, stirring only enough to moisten. Add nuts. Pour into 2 well greased pans. Bake at 325° F. for approximately one hour. Test for doneness with toothpick.

Brick Oven Bread

An old recipe, dating back to days when baking was done in outdoor oven where fire was built right in the oven, and then the hot coals were scraped back and the bread was put in to bake. Of course, the recipe has been modernized so you can bake this right in a 375° F. oven.

INGREDIENTS:

3	cups warm water		1/2	cup sunflower seeds
1	Tbs molasses (or honey)		1/2	cup bran
1/4	cup honey		1/8	tsp cinnamon
2	Tbs yeast		1/3	cup oil
1-1/2	Tbs salt		3/4	cup oatmeal
4	cups white flour		1/4	cup cornmeal
1	egg yolk		1	Tbs water
1	cup W. wheat flour			Sesame seeds

METHOD:

In large bowl mix water, molasses and honey. Sprinkle yeast on mix. Stir lightly to dissolve. Stir in oatmeal, cornmeal, W. wheat flour, sunflower seeds and bran. Cover with cloth and let rise 30 minutes. Stir in cinnamon, oil and salt. Add flour one cup at a time. Knead for approximately 10 minutes, until dough is elasticy and does not stick to hands. Do not add more than 2 cups extra flour. Put in mixing bowl, brush top lightly with oil. Cover and let rise until double in bulk. Punch down and form 2 loaves. Place in greased 9" x 5" x 3" pans. Let rise again (optional). Brush loaves with wash made from egg and water. Sprinkle with seeds. Bake 40 to 50 minutes in 375° F. oven or until done.

French Bread

This recipe calls for more salt than necessary, unless you want a really salty French Bread. Cut down, or omit, according to your taste and diet requirements.

INGREDIENTS:

<u>(A)</u>
1-1/2 tsp dry yeast
1   Tbs honey
1   Tbs sea salt
2   cups hot water
<u>(B)</u>
6 to 7 cups flour

METHOD:

Mix "A" in bowl. Mix in first 5 cups of "B". Spread 6th cup on board: dump batter onto board and knead with as much additional flour as required to stop sticking. Knead another 10 minutes after all the flour is in. Return to bowl, cover and set to rise. When sufficiently risen, punch down; knead out larger air bubbles. Cut the dough into 4 pieces; shape into loaves. Place on baking sheets that have been greased and sprinkled with corn meal. Cover and let rise until double. Slash loaves and sprinkle with water. Boil water and put in pan on bottom of oven. DO NOT preheat oven. Bake at 400°F. for 40 minutes. Sprinkle with water again after 10 or 15 minutes of baking. (Sprinkling makes a crustier bread.)

Honey Bran Squares

A great after-school treat that will bring all the friends over, too.

INGREDIENTS:

1/4	cup honey
1/4	cup butter or margarine, melted
4	cups miniature marshmallows
6	cups favorite bran cereal
1	cup peanuts

METHOD:

Blend honey and butter in large saucepan; stir in marshmallows. Cook and stir over medium-high heat until marshmallows are melted. Mix cereal and nuts; stir in marshmallow mixture until well coated. Press into lightly greased 13" x 9" x 2" pan. Cut into squares. Makes 24 (2" x 2") squares. Preparation Time: About 15 minutes.

Crusty Honey Whole Wheat Bread

No additives, no preservatives and pure honey make this a very healthy bread.

INGREDIENTS:

1	cup milk		1	cup water
1/2	cup honey		3	Tbs butter
2-1/2	cups whole wheat flour		2	packages yeast
1	egg		1	Tbs salt
3-3/4 to 4 cups flour				

METHOD:

Heat milk, water, honey and butter to 120° F. Add yeast. Mix in bowl, 2 to 3 cups white flour, 1 cup wheat flour, egg, salt and milk mixture. Add remaining whole wheat flour and white flour, to form a stiff dough. Place in greased bowl and let rise. Divide and put into 2 loaf pans. Rise and bake at 375° F.

Honey Whole Wheat Bread

Wildflower honey or any darker honey can be substituted for buckwheat honey in this bread.

INGREDIENTS:

1/2	cup uncooked bulgur wheat
2	pkgs dry yeast
1/2	cup instant nonfat dry milk powder
2	Tbs vegetable oil
4-1/2	cups whole wheat flour, divided
	Vegetable cooking spray

1	cup boiling water
1-1/2	cups warm water
1/3	cup plus 1 tbs buckwheat honey
1-1/2	tsps salt
1	cup bread flour

METHOD:

Combine bulgur wheat and boiling water in a large bowl and let stand 30 minutes. Dissolve yeast in 1-1/2 cups warm water. Add milk powder, 1/3 cup honey, oil and salt; let stand 5 minutes. Add to bulgur mixture and stir well. Add 2 cups whole wheat flour and bread flour; beat at high speed in electric mixer 5 minutes. Cover and let rest 15 minutes. Stir in 2 cups whole wheat flour to form a moderately stiff dough. Turn onto bread board and knead for 10 minutes. Place in oiled bowl, cover and place in warm place until doubled in bulk. Knead again for 5 minutes. Place in sprayed bread pans and let rise again. Bake in 350° F. oven until bread shrinks from sides of pan and has crisp top crust. Cool on rack.

Honey Date Nut Bread

There's nothing tricky about cooking Honey Nut Bread in a can. Create your own round baking tins by washing out empty soup or fruit cans and lightly greasing the inside walls. Fill the cans with dough and place upright on a cookie sheet or directly on the oven rack. After baking, gently slide the round loaf onto a serving plate, let cool and slice . Clean-up is nearly non-existent; toss the used cans or simply wipe them clean for future use.

Honey Nut Bread is convenient; make several loaves at a time and freeze. It's a perfect pop-in-the-toaster breakfast starter, a mid-morning take the edge off or, a dinner time main dish accompaniment. A wrapped loaf or two of this naturally sweet bread makes a welcome hostess gift or a special treat for a neighbor or friend.

INGREDIENTS:

1	cup <u>each</u> all-purpose flour and whole wheat flour
1/2	tsp salt
1/2	cup honey
1	egg

1	tsp <u>each</u> baking powder, baking soda and ground cinnamon
1	cup buttermilk
1/4	cup vegetable oil
1/2	cup <u>each</u> pitted, chopped dates and chopped pecans

METHOD:

Combine flours, baking powder, baking soda and salt in large mixing bowl; set aside. Beat buttermilk, honey, vegetable oil and egg until well blended; stir into dry ingredients. Fold in dates and nuts. Pour into 16-ounce round tins. Bake at 350° F. 35 to 40 minutes or until wooden pick inserted in center comes out clean. Makes 3 round loaves.

Honey Raisin Oatmeal Bread

The ingredients in oats that helps lower cholesterol has been identified, so you can know that this bread is good for you.

INGREDIENTS:

2	cups milk		1/2	cup honey
1	pkg dry yeast		2	cups rolled oats
1	Tbs salt		1	tsp cinnamon (optional)
1/4	cup warm water		5	cups flour
1	egg		1	cup raisins
4	Tbs butter or margarine			

METHOD:

Scald milk. Stir in oats, honey, salt, butter and cinnamon. Cool to lukewarm. Sprinkle yeast over warm water. Add dissolved yeast and raisins to mix. Add flour, except 1 cup. Add more flour if necessary to handle dough. Knead until smooth and pliable. Place in lightly greased bowl, turn dough . Cover and let rise in warm place until doubled (1 to 1-1/2 hours). Punch down, and let double again— about 30 minutes. Divide dough into three pieces, let rest 10 minutes and shape into 3 loaves and fit into greased loaf pans. Let rise until double again. Bake at 350° F. for about 40 minutes. Cover with foil last 15 minutes to prevent over-browning. Remove from oven, brush with glaze of 1 Tbs honey, 1 Tbs butter, mixed. Return to oven for 1 minute to harden glaze.

Mixed Grain Bread

Make either bread or rolls. Any kind of vegetable oil can be used, and if you wish, you can cut the salt or use kelp powder instead.

INGREDIENTS:

1/2	cup warm water		2	Tbs dry yeast
1	tsp honey		3	cups whole wheat flour
1	cup rye flour		1	tsp salt (or kelp)
2	Tbs lecitin granules		1/2	cup powdered milk
1	cup hot water		1	cup oatmeal
3/4	cup honey		1/2	cup cold-pressed oil
2	eggs			

METHOD:

Mix 1/2 cup warm water, dry yeast and 1 tsp honey in small bowl and let stand 10 minutes. Combine whole wheat flour, rye flour, salt, lecitin and powdered milk; let set in warm place. Combine in larger bowl: oatmeal, hot water and 3/4 cup honey. Add oil and eggs. Stir in yeast mixture. Stir in dry ingredients until thoroughly combined. Add more whole wheat flour if needed, but dough should be sticky and soft. Cover and let rise 30 minutes. Punch down. Let rise another 30 minutes. Punch down and turn into floured board. Knead for 3 to 5 minutes. Return to oiled bowl. Cover and let rise until double in bulk. Punch down and let set while greasing 2 bread pans or cookie sheets (for rolls or buns). Shape into loaves. Let rise until double. Bake at 350° F. 45 minutes for small loaves, 55 minutes for large loaves, 25-30 for rolls.

Oatmeal Bread

If you want hot bread for dinner, you can mix this dough in the morning and let it rest in the refrigerator until you are ready to start dinner.

INGREDIENTS:

2	cups scalded milk		1	cup oatmeal
2	Tbs butter		2	tsp salt
2	pkgs dry yeast		1/2	cup warm water
1	Tbs honey		1	egg
4-1/2	cups flour, (may need 1/2 cup more if you are not using steel-cut oatmeal)			

METHOD:

Combine scalded milk and oatmeal; add butter and salt and cool 1 hour. Dissolve yeast in warm water, adding honey. Add egg to oatmeal mixture, beating well. Now add yeast mixture. Slowly add 2-1/2 cups flour, beating well; keep adding flour until the dough pulls away from the side of the bowl. Knead dough for a few minutes and put into a greased bowl; set in warm place for 20 minutes. Punch down and divide into 2 well-greased loaf pans. Cover with greased wax paper or plastic wrap and refrigerate 2 to 24 hours. When ready to bake, remove paper and let set at room temperature for 10 minutes. Bake at 400° F. for 35 to 40 minutes.

Honey Cracked Wheat Bread

This bread is good and good for you.

INGREDIENTS:

3	cups warm water
1	Tbs dry yeast
1/3	cup honey
3/4	cup cracked wheat
1	tsp salt
3/4	cup rye flour
7 to 8	cups unbleached wheat flour

METHOD:

Dissolve yeast, honey and salt in warm water. Add cracked wheat. Let stand until bubbly. Add flours until kneadable. Knead for 5 to 10 minutes. let stand and double in bulk. Punch down. Knead 3 to 5 minutes more. Shape into 2 loaves. Let rise until double in bulk. Bake at 350° F. for 35 to 45 minutes.

Honey French Toast

The honey is incorporated right into the toast. A nice variation for a breakfast treat.

INGREDIENTS:

2   eggs, well beaten
1/4   cup milk
1/4   cup honey
1/4   tsp salt
6-8   slices of bread
         Butter

METHOD:

Combine eggs, milk, honey and salt. Dip bread slices into honey mixture. Fry in butter or oil over medium heat until golden brown. Serves 3 to 4.

Honey Braid Bread

Modern technology steps in to make this savory bread easy by using a hot roll mix. The dough is used to weave and enclose honey, walnuts, sun-dried tomatoes and spices, forming an impressive and festive dining centerpiece.

INGREDIENTS:

1-1/2	tsp dried thyme, divided		1	pkg (16 oz) hot roll mix
1/2	cup sun-dried tomatoes			Warm water
1	cup chopped onion		1	clove garlic, minced
1	Tbs olive oil		1/3	cup chopped walnuts
4	Tbs honey, divided		1	Tbs cider vinegar
1	Tbs flour		1/2	tsp salt
	Pepper to taste		1	Tbs water

METHOD:

Add 1 tsp thyme to hot roll mix; prepare dough according to package directions. Cover kneaded dough with bowl and let rest 5 minutes. Cover tomatoes with warm water; let stand 10 to 15 minutes and drain. Dice into 1/2" pieces. Saute onion and garlic in oil until onion softens. Add dice tomatoes, walnuts, 2 Tbs honey, vinegar, flour , remaining thyme, salt and pepper; mix well. Roll dough to 14" x 12 " rectangle on floured board; transfer to greased baking sheet. Make 2-1/2 inch cuts at 1-1/2 inch intervals along both sides of dough., Spread filling down center of dough. Lift strips from each side, crisscrossing them, carefully enclosing filling. Bake at 350° F. for 25 to 30 minutes or until browned. Combine remaining honey and water; mix well. Brush top of braid with honey mixture before cooling. Makes 14 to 16 slices.

Honey Zucchini Bread

Walnuts or filberts are nuts of choice for this recipe. Pecans are also good. If bread browns too fast, lay foil loosely over top of pan during last 15 minutes of baking. Nutmeg can be substituted for cinnamon.

INGREDIENTS:

3	eggs		2	cups grated zucchini (unpeeled)
1	cup honey		3	cups all-purpose flour
3	tsp vanilla		1	tsp soda
1	cup chopped nuts		1/2	tsp baking powder
1/2	tsp cinnamon		1/2	tsp salt
			1	cup vegetable oil

METHOD:

In a large bowl, mix beaten eggs, oil, honey and vanilla. In second bowl, mix dry ingredients and add to egg mix, stirring only enough to moisten. Add nuts and pour into well-greased loaf pans and bake at 325° F. for one hour.

Honey Pineapple Bread

Bake in a loaf pan. This is a nice change from banana bread.

INGREDIENTS:

2	Tbs oil		1	cup honey
1	slightly beaten egg		1/2	tsp salt
1	cup pineapple juice		2	cups unsifted flour
2	tsp baking powder		2	cups whole bran
3/4	cup chopped walnuts			

METHOD:

Mix liquid ingredients. Add dry ingredients, mixing just until moistened. Fold in 3/4 cup chopped walnuts. Pour into greased 5" x 9" loaf pan and bake at 350° F. for one hour or until toothpick tests clean.

Bath Buns

This recipe is said to have originated in Bath, England, one of the British towns where the remnants of the conquering Romans is still most visible.

INGREDIENTS:

2	scant Tbs dry yeast	1/2	cup warm milk
2	eggs, lightly beaten	1/2	tsp salt
2	Tbs honey	3-1/2	cups flour (1/2 cup whole wheat and
	Pinch of saffron, or raisins, cinnamon,		the rest unbleached)
	allspice, currants, candied orange		

METHOD:

Dissolve the yeast in the milk. Stir in the remaining ingredients and knead. More flour has to be added, but add as little as possible. You want a sticky dough. Rise once and form into egg-sized balls. Let rise and bake 15 minutes at 400° F. This is a chewy bun. Really good.

Festive Cream Cheese Rolls

Use your imagination to decorate these rolls. Use nuts, fruit glazes, dried fruits and candy sprinkles, or perhaps a mixture of herbs and pine nuts.

INGREDIENTS:

1/2	cup warm water	2	pkgs dry yeast
1/2	cup milk, scalded and cooled	1/2	cup honey
1-1/2	tsp salt	2	eggs
1/2	cup shortening (or margarine)	5-1/2	cups flour
	Honey cream cheese filling (recipe follows)		

METHOD:

Dissolve yeast in water, Add cooled milk, honey, salt, eggs and shortening. Mix and add half of flour and mix until smooth. Add remaining flour and knead until smooth. Place in greased bowl, cover and let rise until double. Divide dough into 6 parts. Roll each part into 1/2" thick rectangle. Spread with filling. Roll like jelly roll into 6" long ropes; braid three together for each loaf and place sealed edge down on greased pan. Cover and let rise double. Bake at 350° F. for 30 minutes. After removing from oven, brush with warm honey and decorate.

HONEY CREAM CHEESE FILLING: Combine and mix thoroughly 8 ounces cream cheese, 1/4 cup honey, 1/2 tsp vanilla and 1 tsp lemon juice.

Honey Biscuits

A hot, fluffy biscuit is a treat at any meal. These only need honey and butter added ,at the table.

INGREDIENTS:

2	cups flour
2	tsp baking powder
1/2	tsp salt
1/2	cup margarine or butter (cold)
1/4	cup honey
1	Tbs milk

METHOD:

Sift dry ingredients together. Blend honey and milk. Cut butter or margarine into dry ingredients with pasty blender or 2 knives. (Pea size is fine). Gently mix in honey and milk mix (add a little milk, if needed, until dough barely holds together). Form 6" x 9" rectangle, cut into six squares and then into triangles. Bake in 425° F. oven for 10 to 12 minutes, or until lightly brown.

Honey-Cornmeal Biscuits

You can make your own biscuit mix for this recipe, or use one of the handy ones on the market.

INGREDIENTS:

1-1/3 cups Bisquick™ baking mix
1/2   cup milk
1/2   cup yellow cornmeal
2   Tbs honey

METHOD:

Mix all ingredients until dough forms; beat 30 seconds. Turn dough onto surface dusted with baking mix; gently roll in baking mix to coat. Shape into ball; knead 10 times. Roll 1/2" thick. Cut with 2" cutter dipped in baking mix. Bake on ungreased cookie sheet at 450° F. until golden brown, 8 to 10 minutes. Serve with additional honey or honey butter.
HONEY BUTTER: Beat 1/2 cup margarine or butter, softened, 1/4 cup honey and, if desired, 1/2 tsp grated orange peel until fluffy.
HONEY-CORNMEAL DROP BISCUITS: After beating, drop dough by rounded spoonfuls onto ungreased cookie sheet. Bake until golden brown, 10 to 12 minutes.
HIGH ALTITUDE: Heat oven to 475° F.

Honey Corn Sticks

Make these for dinner and serve warm with honey butter!

INGREDIENTS:

1	cup unsifted flour		1	cup yellow cornmeal
1	Tbs baking powder		1/2	tsp salt
1	cup milk		1	egg or 2 whites
2	Tbs honey		1	Tbs butter or margarine
1/4	cup fresh chives or 4 tsp dried (other herbs can be substituted)			

METHOD:

Heat oven to 425° F. Heat cast iron corn ear pan and grease. Combine flour, cornmeal, baking powder and salt. Mix egg, honey, milk, margarine and chives; stir into flour mix, blend well and fill pan mold almost full. Bake 15 minutes.

Honey Oat Biscotti

The beneficial ingredient of oats has been identified. Eat them for health. These cookies are good, too!

INGREDIENTS:

1/2	cup butter or margarine		3/4	cup honey
2	eggs		1	tsp vanilla
2	cups flour		3	tsp ground cinnamon
1	tsp baking powder		1/2	tsp each baking soda and salt
2	cups rolled oats		1/2	cup chopped nuts

METHOD:

Cream butter; beat in honey, eggs and vanilla. Combine flour, cinnamon. baking powder, baking soda and salt; mix well. Stir into butter mixture. Stir in oats and nuts. On greased baking sheet shape dough into 2 (10" x 3" x 1" each) logs. Bake at 350° F. 12 to 15 minutes or until lightly browned. Cool 5 minutes; remove to cutting board. Cut each log into 1/2" strips; place in cookie sheet. Bake at 300° F. 25 to 30 minutes or until crisp throughout strip. Cool thoroughly. Makes 3 dozen cookies. Preparation Time: About 15 minutes. Baking Time: about 45 minutes.

Brown Honey Scones

A different kind of scone, but a very good one.

INGREDIENTS:

3   cups whole wheat flour
3   tsp baking powder
1/2   tsp salt
1   Tbs butter
2   Tbs honey
1   cup milk

METHOD:

Mix flour, baking powder and salt. Rub in butter. Dissolve honey in the milk and mix to a soft dough, using a knife for mixing . Knead lightly. Roll and pat out 3/4" thickness. Cut into 2" squares and place on a cold tray. Bake at 425° F. for 10 to 12 minutes.

Honey Orange Rolls

Orange rolls like these made with honey are a treat for breakfast, after school or a bed-time snack.

INGREDIENTS:

1	cup orange juice, warmed		1/4	cup butter
1/4	cup honey		1/4	cup brown sugar
1-1/2	tsp salt		2	eggs
1/2	cup warm water		4-1/4 to 4-3/4 cups flour
1	cup rolled oats		2	tsp grated orange peel
2	pkgs dry yeast			

METHOD:

Combine orange juice, butter, honey, sugar and salt. Stir to melt butter. Dissolve yeast in water; combine with juice mixture. Add oats, orange peel and enough flour to make a soft dough. Knead on lightly floured board until smooth and satiny, about 10 minutes. Cover and let rise until double, about 1 hour. Punch down. Shape into 24 rolls and place in greased muffin tins. Cover and let rise until nearly double, about 45 minutes. (If you like, brush tops with melted butter before baking.) Bake in 375° F. oven for about 30 minutes.

Carrot Honey Bran Muffins

Any dark flavored honey can be used in place of buckwheat honey. Try some different ones to find the flavor just right for you.

INGREDIENTS:

1-1/2	cup whole wheat flour		1	tsp salt (optional)
1-1/2	cups unprocessed bran		1/2	tsp nutmeg
1	tsp cinnamon		1-1/2	tsp baking soda
2	Tbs vinegar		1/2	cup honey
2	eggs		1-1/2	cups milk
1	cup finely grated carrots		1/4	cup oil
1/4	cup buckwheat honey		1	currants (optional)

METHOD:

Mix 6 dry ingredients together in large bowl. Mix all remaining ingredients in another bowl. Combine and mix just until dry ingredients are moistened. Fill muffin pans 3/4 full. Bake at 325° F. for 20 to 35 minutes.

Overnight Rolls

There are lots of faster ways to make rolls, but you may want to try this recipe when you are going to be home all day and want some hot rolls for breakfast the next morning.

INGREDIENTS:

4	cups boiling water		2	heaping Tbs shortening
1-1/2	cups honey		1	Tbs salt
3	eggs		1	pkg dry yeast
6	cups whole wheat flour		6 to 7	cups white flour

METHOD:

Cool 1/2 cup water to lukewarm, add 2 tsp of sugar and dissolve yeast in it. Add shortening and honey to rest of water and cool to lukewarm (stir to dissolve). Beat eggs with salt; add to rest of liquid ingredients and the whole wheat flour. Beat. Add one cup remaining flour at a time. Put into greased bowl, let rise, kneading every one half hour. Mix between 5 and 8 in the evening. Around 10:00 p.m., shape into buns and let rise overnight. In morning, bake in 350° F. oven about 15 minutes. Grease tops with butter or margarine.

Honey Crunch Loaf

No time to bake? This Honey Crunch Loaf to the rescue.

INGREDIENTS:

1	round loaf, unsliced white bread
1/2	cup butter or margarine, melted
1/2	cup honey, divided
1/2	cup sugar-coated cereal
1/2	cup flaked coconut
1/2	cup brown sugar

METHOD:

Slice bread almost to the bottom, 4 or 5 times in each direction. Place loaf on piece of foil on baking sheet; turn up edges of of foil. Combine the butter or margarine with 1/4 cup of honey; spoon over top of loaf and let excess drizzle between sections. Combine cereal, coconut and brown sugar; sprinkle on top of loaf and between section. Drizzle with the remaining 1/4 cup of honey. Heat at 350° F. for 20 minutes or until lightly browned.

Honey Fruit Rolls

For breakfast, lunch, dinner, or a snack — you can't beat these rolls, and they are easy to fix.

INGREDIENTS:

1	package roll mix
1/4	cup butter
1/2	cup honey
1/4	cup chopped dried fruit (dates, raisins, prunes)
1/2	cup chopped nuts

METHOD:

Cream butter, add honey gradually and blend well. Add chopped nuts and dried fruit. Roll out biscuits or yeast roll dough and spread with filling. Roll up carefully, slice and bake according to package directions.

Honey Cinnamon Buns

An old favorite with an extra bit of the good flavor of honey.

INGREDIENTS:

2/3	cup very warm water	1	Tbs yeast
1/2	cup cinnamon honey butter (recipe follows)	1	egg
1/2	tsp salt	2	Tbs nonfat milk
1/4	cup raisins	1/2	cup chopped walnuts
2	cups sifted flour		

METHOD:

Measure warm water into large bowl. Sprinkle yeast over water to dissolve. Combine cinnamon, honey butter, egg, salt and dry milk. Add yeast to mix. Blend well. Add fruit, nuts and flour. Stir about 2 minutes. Cover and let rise until double in bulk. Stir down and drop by spoonfuls into 12 greased muffin cups. Let rise again until doubled. Bake 20 to 25 minutes in 350° F. oven. Serve warm with additional cinnamon honey butter.

CINNAMON HONEY BUTTER: Cream together 1/4 cup margarine or butter, 1/2 cup honey and 1 tsp cinnamon. (Try ginger butter, too, by adding 1 tsp dried ginger in place of cinnamon.)

Honey Marinade for Meats

Honey
It's a Natural

For thousands of years, people have loved honey. And it's always been produced in the same way - in one of the most efficient factories in the world - the bee hive. From fields of clover... from citrus orchards... from mountain wild flowers, honey bees collect nectar to create pure, wholesome, delicious honey.

The color and flavor of honeys differ depending on the blossoms visited by the honey bees. The color ranges from water white to dark amber and the flavor varies from delectably mild to distinctly bold.

No matter what color and flavor, honey is the sweetener of choice for today's busy chef. Honey's sweetness is a natural not only on toast for breakfast, but as an ingredient in all sorts of recipes. Honey adds golden color, flavor and body to a variety of simple sauces, dips and toppings. So spread the news - honey's a natural.

Frequent Flyer
Honey bees will fly over 55,000 miles to bring you one pound of honey.

Busy Bees
An average worker bee will visit 50 to 100 flowers on each collection trip. Yet in her lifetime, the busy bee will gather enough nectar to make only 1/12 of a teaspoon of honey.

Creme de la Creme
Creme or spun honey is finely crystallized honey. While all honey will crystallize in time, the crystallization of cremed honey is controlled so that at room temperature it can be spread like butter on toast., biscuits or muffins.

Favorite Entrees
and
Marinades and Sauces

Western Light Broil

Use either round or top sirloin and don't overcook!

INGREDIENTS:

1-1/2	lbs beef round steak
1	green onion and top, chopped
2	Tbs lemon juice
1	garlic clove, crushed

1/2	cup soy sauce
1/4	cup water
2	Tbs honey
2	tsp toasted sesame seeds

METHOD:

Score top of steak in a diamond pattern, cutting 1/2 inch deep. place steak in a flat glass dish. Combine all ingredients, pour over steak and cover. Marinate 24 - 48 hours in the refrigerator. Turn several times. Broil to rare or medium, brushing with marinade. To serve, slice steak across grain into thin slices.

Thick Spare Ribs

Don't have the fire too hot. These ribs need to cook slowly. Brush the marinade on them several times as they cook.

INGREDIENTS:

1	cup soy sauce
1	cup honey
1	cup crushed pineapple
2	sliced lemons
4	tsp preserved candied ginger
1	cup white wine vinegar
8	garlic cloves (chopped)

METHOD:

Mix all ingredients together. Marinate thick spare ribs at least an hour, but can leave in the sauce over night. Broil the ribs one hour.

Honey and Wine Ribs

This is a different way to prepare short or spare ribs. They will be tender and good.

INGREDIENTS:

4	lbs short or spare ribs		1	8 oz can tomato sauce
1/4	cup red wine		1/2	cup honey
1/4	cup red wine vinegar		1	Tbs instant minced onions
1	tsp onion salt		1	tsp garlic salt
1	tsp ground cloves			

METHOD:

Broil ribs under broiler for 30 minutes, turning occasionally, to brown and remove excess fat. Place ribs in casserole. Combine remaining ingredients and pour over ribs. Place covered casserole in a 325° F. oven for approximately 1 hour.

Barbecued Beef Short Ribs

Once you have tasted these you will never want to have short ribs without honey again.

INGREDIENTS:

3	lbs beef short ribs
1/2	cup water
1/2	cup catsup
1/2	cup onion (finely chopped)
2	Tbs Worcestershire sauce
1	Tbs honey
2	tsp prepared mustard

METHOD:

Brown ribs in skillet, cover tightly and cook slowly for 1 hour. Pour off drippings. Add water to ribs. Cover tightly and cook until tender. Combine catsup, honey, mustard, vinegar, onions and Worcestershire sauce for barbecue sauce. Remove ribs from skillet, place on rack in broiler pan, brush ribs with sauce, place broiler pan 3 to 4 inches from source of heat. Broil about 5 minutes or until browned. Turn and brush other side with remaining sauce, continue to broil for 2 to 3 minutes. 4 servings.

Hawaiian Nuggets

Chicken or turkey nuggets can be used, or cut skinned chicken or turkey into small pieces for this dish.

INGREDIENTS:

1	cup honey	1/2	tsp ginger
1/2	tsp salt	1/4	cup sherry
1/2	cup chopped green onions	1/2	chopped celery
1	cup pineapple tid bits	1	cup pineapple juice
1	Tbs cornstarch dissolved in 2 tsp cold water		

METHOD:

Combine all ingredients except cornstarch and bring to boil. Cook 10 minutes. Add cornstarch and boil again to thicken. Heat oven to 400° F. Cook chicken or turkey for 12 minutes. Remove from oven and place in baking dish. Pour sauce over top. Return to oven for 12 more minutes at 350° F. Serve over rice.

Sweet and Sour Chicken Wings

If you are making appetizers for a crowd, you can double or triple the recipe.

INGREDIENTS:

WINGS
1	frying chicken, 3 to 4 Lbs cut into serving pieces
1	cup flour
1/4	tsp salt
1	large egg
1/8	tsp pepper
1	tsp water

SAUCE
1	cup chicken broth either canned, bouillon cube or made from stock
1/2	cup catsup
1	Tbs soy sauce
1/2	cup honey
1/4	cup vinegar
1	tsp oil or shortening for browning

METHOD:

If making chicken stock, simmer together neck, wing tips and back with 1/2 cup chopped celery, 1 tsp minced onion, 1/4 tsp salt, dash garlic salt, dash pepper and 2 cups water. Simmer 1 hour. Rinse chicken pieces with water, drain. Beat egg, water and oil. Pour over chicken. Dip pieces into seasoned flour mix. Heat oil in skillet and brown chicken. Remove to shallow covered baking dish. (May use 9" x 13" glass pan covered with foil.) To make sauce, pour off all oil from skillet and combine chicken broth with catsup, soy sauce, honey and vinegar. Heat slowly until honey is dissolved. Pour over chicken and bake at 350° F. for 45 minutes. Remove cover and baste sauce over chicken or turn pieces over in sauce. Continue baking uncovered 15 minutes longer. May serve with hot rice. Serves 5 to 6.

Honey Sauce

This sauce can be poured over plain cooked rice, or you can add shrimp to the rice if you want to make it a main course.

INGREDIENTS:

1/3	cup cold water
1-1/2	Tbs corn starch
1	Tbs chicken bouillon
1	tsp sesame oil
1/2	tsp garlic powder
3	Tbs honey

METHOD:

Mix water and corn starch thoroughly in small saucepan. Add other ingredients and stir until blended. Heat on medium until mixture thickens. Cook 1 minute . Add crushed drained pineapples and pour over hot rice.

Chicken and Glaze

This recipe is for 24 hungry picnickers if you serve each a half chicken.

INGREDIENTS:

1/2	cup oil
3/4	cup lemon juice
2	Tbs Tabasco
1	tsp Worchestershire sauce
1	tsp salt
1/4	cup honey
24	half chickens or large pieces

METHOD:

Mix all ingredients well. Rotate chicken on basket rotisserie about an hour and a half, during the last 20 minutes, brush the chicken frequently with sauce for a beautiful glaze and excellent flavor.

Honey Fried Chicken

Fried chicken is always better if one takes a few extra minutes to give it a tasty coating. Honey is the ingredient that adds a special touch to this fried chicken.

INGREDIENTS:

3	Lbs cut-up chicken
3/4	cup honey
3/4 to 1	cup buttermilk baking mix
2	tsp dry mustard
1/2	tsp paprika
	Vegetable oil
	salt and pepper to taste

METHOD:

Coat chicken with honey; set aside. Combine buttermilk, baking mix, mustard, paprika, salt and pepper: dredge chicken in mixture. Heat 1/2" oil to 375° F. in 12" skillet over medium heat. Carefully place chicken in hot oil and cook about 5 minutes or until under side of chicken is golden; turn chicken pieces and cook about 5 minutes, turning as needed. Reduce heat to low and cook 7 to 10 minutes longer or until chicken tests done and juices run clear. Remove chicken; drain on paper towels. Repeat with remaining chicken pieces. Makes 4 to 6 servings.

TIP: Chicken can be browned in hot oil, placed on baking sheet and baked at 350° F. 20 to 30 minutes or until chicken tests done and juices run clear.

Oven Barbecued Chicken

Serves five or six.

INGREDIENTS:

3	Lb fryer
1/2	cup salad dressing
1/4	cup melted butter
1/4	cup hot ketchup
1	Tbs lemon juice
2	Tbs honey
1	Tbs paprika

METHOD:

Season chicken. Combine all ingredients in baking pan. Arrange chicken in a single layer. Turn once to coat. Bake at 350° F. for 45 to 60 minutes or until done, basting every 15 minutes. Serves 5 or 6

Honey-Pineapple Stir-Fry

A quick, delicious dinner. Just add a salad and dessert.

INGREDIENTS:

STIR-FRY
2	cups cubed chicken or turkey
3 to 5	cups cut vegetables
1	cup celery
1	stalk broccoli, cut 3/4" x 1/4"
1	large onion, cut in 1/2" wedges
1/2	green pepper, chopped
1	cup zucchini, 1-1/2" x 1/4"
5	carrots, 1" x 1/4"
1	can (20 oz) pineapple, drained (crushed or chunks)
	Topping, sliced almonds and sesame seeds

HONEY SAUCE
3/4	cups water
1-1/2	Tbs corn starch
1	Tbs instant chicken bouillon
1	tsp sesame oil
1/2	tsp garlic powder
3	Tbs honey

METHOD:

Stir-fry meat, remove, add 1 Tbs oil, cook onion until clear. Add green pepper, cook together and remove. Stir-fry carrots, broccoli, cook tender-crisp, remove, Stir-fry celery until tender-crisp, add zucchini, cook 2 minutes. Put all cooked ingredients into wok, stir together. Add HONEY SAUCE. Add pineapple (mix in 2 tsp ginger powder). Cook until thickened, a few minutes. Pour over hot rice, top with topping.

Honey of a Mandarin Chicken

Now that we are all eating more chicken and fish, a variety of good chicken recipes, like this one, is handy.

INGREDIENTS:

6	chicken breasts	1	can (11 oz) mandarin oranges
1	egg, beaten	3/4	cup flour
3	Tbs honey	1/2	cup oil
2	Tbs brown sugar	1	can (14 oz) can chunk pineapple
1	cup orange juice	3	Tbs cornstarch and 1/2 cup water to mix

METHOD:

Dip chicken in beaten egg, salt, pepper, and flour. Heat pan with oil and lightly brown chicken, Remove to casserole dish. Preheat oven to 350° F. In saucepan, combine juice from pineapple, oranges, and orange juice with honey and brown sugar. When hot, mix cornstarch with water and stir in juices. Cook until it begins to thicken. Remove from heat. Arrange pineapple chunks and oranges around chicken pieces. Pour juice mixture over top and bake at 350° F. for 1 hour, longer if large chicken parts. Serve over a bed of rice.

Game Hens with Honey Cilantro Marinade

This recipe is equally good with any kind of poultry. Vary grilling time according to size of pieces, and by testing (cooked poultry is no longer pink when cut at thickest part).

INGREDIENTS:

2 to 4	Cornish game hens
2	tsp dry mustard
4	cloves minced garlic
2	Tbs soy sauce
3	Tbs honey
1/4	cup marsala wine or apple juice
2/3	cup minced fresh cilantro (coriander) or 1/3 cup dry cilantro

METHOD:

Rinse game hens and split lengthwise with poultry or kitchen shears, so hens lie flat. Make marinade by combining all ingredients and bringing to a boil. Cool and place hens and marinade in plastic bag. Chill for an hour or more. Place hens, skin side up on grill 4 to 6 inches from bed of medium coals. Cook, turning often and basting with marinade. Test for doneness.

Pineapple Mustard Pork Chops

Give new life to pork chops with this combination of pineapple , mustard and honey.

INGREDIENTS:

8	boneless pork chops
1/2	cup velvety pineapple honey mustard (recipe follows)
1	cup fresh bread crumbs
1	tsp fresh chopped sage or 1/3 tsp dry ground sage

METHOD:

Velvety pineapple mustard - Soak 1/2 cup dry mustard in 1/3 cup pineapple juice. In a saucepan, heat until thick, 1 cup pineapple juice, 1/2 tsp salt, 1/2 cup honey, 1/3 cup vinegar. Cool and add the mustard and pineapple mix. Trim fat from meat, and cover with mustard sauce. Dredge in bread crumbs and sage. Bake in 375° F. oven for 25 minutes, or until no longer pink, or until no longer pink in the center. Serve with rest of velvety pineapple honey mustard sauce.

Honey Baked Chicken

A main course for tonight's dinner? Thaw some frozen chicken in the microwave, and use this recipe.

INGREDIENTS:

1/4	cup melted butter
1/2	cup honey
1/4	cup prepared mustard
1	tsp salt
1	tsp curry powder

METHOD:

Mix the 5 ingredients together well and pour over 5 to 6 pieces of cut-up chicken in a 9" x 9" x 2" pan. Bake at 325° F. for 75 minutes. Baste occasionally.

Sucre et amer a l'envers Cordon Blue
(Sweet and sour inside and out cordon blue)

INGREDIENTS:

BUFFET FARE		SWEET & SOUR SAUCE	
24	slices of ham	1/3	cup honey
48	pieces sliced Swiss cheese (1" x 1/2")	1/3	cup pineapple juice
1	chicken breast cut into 24 pieces	1/4	cup vinegar
24	toothpicks	1	Tbs soy sauce
		1	Tbs corn starch

METHOD:

Place each piece of chicken between 2 slices of cheese. Place each piece in corner of a slice of ham and roll up like egg roll. Secure with toothpick. Combine all Sweet and Sour Sauce ingredients in saucepan and cook until the starch is set. Cover chicken pieces with Sweet and Sour Sauce and cook in microwave for 5 to 6 minutes

Honey Fruited Pork Chops

Serves four.

INGREDIENTS:

4	double loin pork chops
1/4	cup pineapple syrup
1	can (8-1/2 oz) sliced pineapple
1	tsp prepared mustard
1/2	cup honey
	Maraschino cherries

METHOD:

Cut pocket into each chop and insert a half slice of pineapple. Combine honey, pineapple syrup and mustard and spoon a little over each chop. Bake at 350° F. for 1-1/2 hors, drizzling honey sauce over the chops frequently. Remove chops form oven. Top each with 1/2 slice of pineapple and a maraschino cherry. Return to oven briefly to warm the fruit. Heat any remaining honey sauce and serve with chops. Makes four servings.

Speedy Grilled Chicken with Honey-Orange Glaze

It's always nice to have a different way to jazz up chicken on top. This is a favorite.

INGREDIENTS:

1/4	cup honey
2	Tbs orange juice
1	tsp grated orange peel
1/4	tsp dry mustard
1	small clove garlic, minced
1	(about 3 lb.) cut-up fryer
	Salt and pepper to taste

METHOD:

Blend honey, orange juice, peel, mustard and garlic; salt and pepper to taste. Rinse chicken pieces; pat dry. Arrange in microwave- safe dish with thicker pieces to the edge. Microcook at HIGH (100%) 15 minutes. Remove to grill and cook, skin side down, 5 minutes; turn and grill 5 to 10 minutes or until chicken is tender and juices run clear. Brush with sauce just before serving. Preparation Time: Less than 45 minutes.

Honey Pork Chops and Apples

Honey Pork Chops and Apples was a dish chosen as being a representative favorite for the U.S.A. at the recent Goodwill Games.

INGREDIENTS:

6	pork loins chops (about 1/4 inch thick)
2	Granny Smith or other tart apples
1	tsp butter or margarine
1/4	cup honey
6	maraschino cherries
	Salt, pepper and ground sage

METHOD:

Brown chops slowly in skillet; remove to shallow baking dish. Season chops with salt, pepper and sage. Core and slice apples into 1/2-inch rings. Add butter to skillet and saute apple rings until crisp-tender. Place 1 apple ring on to each chop. Cover and bake at 300° F. for 30 minutes. Drizzle honey over apples and chops; baste with drippings. Cover and bake 15 minutes longer or until pork is fully cooked. Place cherry in center of apple rings before serving. Makes six servings.

Honey and Spice Glazed Ham

Honey and ham were made for each other. You can use either canned home or regular ham in this recipe. Vary the amount of glaze according to the size of the ham.

INGREDIENTS:

	Ham (whole or partial)
2	parts Heinz 57 Sauce
1	part honey or 1 part of each

METHOD:

Score whole, half or partial canned ham; stud with whole cloves, if desired. Brush ham with Honey 'N Spice Glaze. Bake ham following package directions, brushing occasionally with glaze during baking.

Zesty Sauce

INGREDIENTS:

1	can (15 oz) or 2 cans (8 oz each) tomato sauce with tomato bits
1	clove garlic, finely minced
2	Tbs diced canned green chilies (or a few drops red pepper sauce)

2	Tbs honey
2	Tbs wine vinegar
2	green onions, finely sliced (tops included)

METHOD:

Combine all ingredients. Heat to use as meat loaf sauce. May be used hot or chill to serve as dip. Makes 2 cups.

Zesty Meat Loaf

A 'different' main course for dinner. The Zesty sauce peps up beef, chicken or shrimp.

INGREDIENTS:

1	egg	1/2	cup milk
1-1/2	tsp salt	1/4	tsp paprika
1/4	tsp ground pepper	3/4	cup white or wheat bread crumbs
1	LB ground chuck or round		Zesty sauce

METHOD:

In a large bowl, beat egg slightly with fork. Add milk, seasonings and bread crumbs. Blend together lightly. Put 1 tsp of Zesty sauce in bottom of 6 (3") muffin cups. Divide meat loaf into each cup. Shape lightly to resemble muffin. Bake at 350° F. (moderate) 20 to 25 minutes or according to how you like your meat. Serve hot with balance of Zesty sauce

Baked Beans with Frankfurters

If you want to serve a crowd of about 100 persons, here is the recipe.

INGREDIENTS:

SWEET AND SOUR HONEY SAUCE

2	cups honey
1-1/2	qts tomato sauce
1/2	cup cider vinegar
1/2	cup soy sauce
2	Tbs dry mustard

BEANS AND FRANKFURTERS

4-1/4	cans (#10) baked beans
2	qts onions, chopped
1	qt green peppers, chopped
6 lbs 4 oz	Frankfurters, cut into chunks

METHOD:

Combine and mix all Sweet and Sour Sauce ingredients. Place 6 qts plus 1-1/3 cups baked beans in each of two 12" x 20" x 4" steamtable pans. Add equal amounts of sauce, onions and green peppers to each pan of beans; mix well and cover. Bake in 350° F. oven one hour. Remove cover and add frankfurters. Bake an additional 30 minutes. Portion with 6 oz ladle (3/4 cup).

Honey Cured Smoked Salmon

For a 10 to 12 pound salmon. Ingredients can be adjusted up or down for size of fish. "Old Bay" seafood seasoning can be used or any assortment of spices using dill, basil, thyme, etc.

INGREDIENTS:

1	quart water
1/2	cup salt
3/4	cup honey
2	Tbs seafood seasoning

METHOD:

Soak salmon in brine mixture of above ingredients for 12 hours in refrigerator. Remove, pat dry and air for one hour. Place in heated smoke house or smoker and smoke with an equal mix of alder and apple chips for 8 hours. (3 to 4 pans of chips dampened.)

Honey Cured Smoked Salmon Omelet

Recipe makes one omelet. Cook each one individually for persons being served.

INGREDIENTS:

3	eggs
1	tsp water
6	drops Tabasco sauce
1	pat butter or margarine
3	Tbs grated swiss cheese
3	Tbs shredded honey cured smoked salmon

METHOD:

Melt butter or margarine in medium-hot omelet pan. Add eggs which have been beaten with water and Tabasco sauce. Cook until eggs are set, tipping pan and lifting edges to evenly cook eggs. When eggs are set, add salmon and cheese, fold and slide onto serving plate.

Kolach

Kolach is traditionally a Polish dish. This recipe gives an easy way to make it.

INGREDIENTS:

1	package (16 oz.) hot roll mix		1/2	cup wheat germ
1	cup warm milk (110° to 114° F.)		2	eggs
2	cups pitted chopped prunes		1	medium orange, unpeeled, chopped (about 2/3 cup)
1/3	cup honey			Honey for glaze optional
3/4	cup water			

METHOD:

Add wheat germ to flour mix. Dissolve yeast in warm milk in large mixer bowl; add eggs and mix well. Beat in flour mixture. Knead dough on floured board until smooth and elastic. Place in greased bowl; let rise until double in bulk. Combine prunes, orange , honey and water in sauce pan. Cook and stir until mixture comes to a boil; simmer 10 minutes or until thickened. Cool. When dough has doubled in bulk, punch down and cut in 18 pieces. Pat dough into 3-inch rounds and place on greased baking sheet. Make indentation in center of each round; fill with heaping tablespoons of cooled prune mixture. Let rise until doubled in bulk. Bake at 350° F. for ten minutes or until dough browns. Brush with honey while still warm, if desired. Makes 1 1/2 dozen.

Honey Sauce

When you want to pep up the rice that you serve with poultry, whip up this sauce and pour over the rice just before it goes to the table.

INGREDIENTS:

3/4	cup cold water
1	tsp sesame oil
1-1/2	Tbs corn starch
1/2	tsp garlic salt
1	Tbs chicken bouillon
3	Tbs honey

METHOD:

Mix water and corn starch thoroughly in small saucepan. Add other ingredients and stir until blended. Heat on medium until mixture thickens. Cool 1 minute. Add crushed, drained pineapple and pour over hot rice.

Chili Sauce

This sauce is handy to have on hand. Use it for chili base, over stuffed green peppers, or add a little more pepper and use on Mexican dishes.

INGREDIENTS:

5-6	qts ripe tomatoes, peeled, chopped or put through colander to remove seeds	2	cups ground green peppers
1-1/2	cups ground onions	2	cups ground red peppers
1	cup mild honey	2	Tbs plain salt
1	tsp cinnamon	1	tsp allspice
		2	cups vinegar

METHOD:

Pour off water from tomatoes, so they will cook down faster. Cook with peppers, onions and salt until thick. Add honey, vinegar, and spice, boil only a short time, to heat through. Ladle into clean sterilized pint jars. Place in canner with water covering the tops and boil 10 minutes to be sure of seal. Remove, cool and store. Makes 8 pints.

Honey Bran Squares

One-Handed Snacks Are
Becoming a Trend

Time-saving and convenience are essential components of today's hectic American lifestyles, and they're having a profound effect on the way we eat.

Sit-down meals are a luxury many people can no longer afford. Grazing is now the national pastime. Whether or not it's in our cars or at our computers, we're eating smaller amounts at more frequent intervals. And, as a result, our latest concern about the food we eat is whether or not it can be eaten with one hand.

With little or no time on work days to use the kitchen as anything more than a warming center, weekends can be spent preparing foods to get us through the week without much additional effort.

Filled with fiber, Honey Bran Squares (page 45) and Honey Oat Biscotti (page 62) are two easy, make-ahead treats that handle well on the road or at the computer. These grazing delicacies can be easily maneuvered from hand to hand, making them a great on-the-go breakfast or anytime snack.

Cakes and Cookies

Granola Bars

You can add your favorite things to this basic recipe.

INGREDIENTS:

3 1/2	cups quick oats (toasted 10 mins. at 350° F.)	
1/2	cup sunflower seeds	
1/3	cup honey	
1/2	tsp salt	

2/3	cups butter or margarine, melted
1/2	cup brown sugar
1	egg, beaten
1/2	tsp vanilla

METHOD:

Combine all ingredients. Add 1/2 cup of favorite fruit (raisins, dates, raspberries, chocolate chips, chopped apples, nuts or 1 Tbs cinnamon). Place mixture in greased 9" x 13" pan. Bake 18 minutes at 350° F. Remove from oven. Cool. Cut into rectangles or use cookie cutter for fun shapes. Makes 2 to 3 dozen bars.

Honey Granola

There many variations of Granola. Ones made with honey are healthy and tasty.

INGREDIENTS:

4	cups old fashioned rolled oats
2	cups coarsely chopped nuts
1	cup golden raisins
3/4	cup honey
1/2	cup butter or margarine
2	tsp ground cinnamon
1	tsp vanilla
	Dash salt

METHOD:

Combine oats, nuts and raisins in large bowl; mix well and set aside. Combine honey, butter, cinnamon, vanilla and salt in saucepan; bring to a boil and cook one minute. Pour honey mixture over oat mixture and toss until well blended. Spread in lightly greased cookie sheet. Bake at 350° F. 20 minutes or until lightly browned; stir every 5 minutes. Cool. Crumble and store in air tight container up to 2 weeks. Makes 8 cups. Preparation Time: Less than 30 minutes.

Honey Bear Bars

These go nicely in lunch boxes, to picnics, or a festive addition to the holiday cookie assortment.

INGREDIENTS:

2	eggs		1/2	cup honey
1	Tbs vegetable oil		1	ripe banana, mashed
2	tsp vanilla		2/3	cup all purpose flour
1/2	cup nonfat dry milk		1/3	cup wheat germ
1	cup snipped dried apricots (about 19)			

METHOD:

Combine eggs, honey, vegetable oil, banana and vanilla and blend well. Combine flour, dry milk, wheat germ and apricots. Stir mixtures together, blending well. Coat 9" square baking pan with non-stick spray. Spread batter in pan and bake in 350° F. oven for 25 to 30 minutes. Cool and cut into 32 bars.

Honey Brownies

The honey in these will keep them fresh longer.

INGREDIENTS:

1/2	cup butter or margarine
2/3	cup honey
2	tsp vanilla
1/2 to 1	tsp ground cinnamon (optional)
1/2	cup chopped nuts (optional)
	Powdered sugar (optional)

4	oz unsweetened baking chocolate
1	egg
1/4	cup flour
1/4	tsp baking soda
	Dash salt

METHOD:

Melt butter and chocolate; stir in honey, egg and vanilla and beat until well mixed. Combine flour, cinnamon, soda and salt; mix well. Add honey to mixture. Stir in nuts. Pour into prepared 9" square baking pan. Bake at 350° F. for 12 minutes or until wooden pick inserted near center comes out clean. DO NOT OVERBAKE. Cut into squares when cool. Sprinkle with powdered sugar if desired. Makes 12 (3" x 2-1/4") pieces.

Fruitcake Cookies

These are glorious gift cookies. They keep well and also freeze well.

INGREDIENTS:

1/4	cup butter
2	eggs
1/2	tsp salt
1/2	tsp <u>each</u> cloves, cinnamon and nutmeg
1	cup glacè cherries
1	cup diced glacè pineapple or mixed glacè fruit

1/2	cup honey
1-1/2	cups sifted flour
1	tsp soda
2	Tbs milk
1	cup seedless raisins
2	cup coarsely chopped walnuts
1/3	cup pineapple juice or dark rum

METHOD:

Cream butter, continue creaming while adding honey in fine stream. Add eggs, beating until well blended. Measure flour; set aside half to coat prepared fruits and nuts. Sift in balance of flour with salt, soda and spices. Add to honey mixture. Add milk. Stir flour coated fruits and nuts into dough. Add pineapple juice. Dough will be soft. It is *important* to chill 1 hour or longer. Drop by rounded teaspoonfuls onto greased baking sheet. Bake at 250° F. (slow) 20 to 25 minutes. *Do not overbake.* Keep remaining dough refrigerated between bakings. Makes 6 dozen.

Coconut Honey Squares

These freeze well. This recipe makes 9 squares, so you can put extras away to serve later.

INGREDIENTS:

1	cup butter or margarine		1	cup honey
1	tsp salt		1	tsp vanilla
1	egg		3/4	cup unsifted flour
1/2	tsp baking powder		1	cup quick cooking oats
1	pkg (4 oz) shredded coconut or 1 can (3-1/2 oz) flaked coconut		1/2	cup coarsely chopped walnuts or pecans

METHOD:

Cream butter, continue creaming while adding honey in a fine stream. Add salt, vanilla and egg and beat until well blended. Sift four with baking powder. Stir in oats, coconut and nuts, mixing thoroughly. Spoon dough into greased 9" square pan. Bake at 350° F. (moderate) 40 to 45 minutes, or until cake tests done. While still warm, cut into squares and serve plain or with honey sweetened whipped cream or softened vanilla ice cream. Makes 9 squares

Coconut Chews

Cookies like these are so good and so easy to make. Bake up some to store in the freezer for lunch boxes, or busy day treats.

INGREDIENTS:

2/3	cup unsweetened condensed milk		2	eggs
1/2	cup honey		1	cup flour
2	Tbs vanilla		1/2	tsp baking soda
1/8	tsp salt		1	tsp baking powder
1/2	cup instant powdered milk		1/4	cup wheat germ
1-1/2	cups coconut			

METHOD:

Mix milk, honey and vanilla. Blend in eggs. Mix flour, baking soda, baking powder, salt, powdered milk and wheat germ. Mix in coconut. Pour into greased, square baking pan and bake at 325° F. for 12 to 15 minutes, or until toothpick comes out clean. Cut into small squares when cooled.

Chocolate Mint Chip Drop Cookies

These are favorites with the younger set.

INGREDIENTS:

2/3	cup butter or margarine		3-1/2	cups flour
1	cup honey		1	tsp baking soda
1/2	cup brown sugar		1/2	tsp salt
2	eggs		1/2	cup chopped walnuts
2	tsp vanilla		1	cup chocolate mint chips

METHOD:

Cream butter, brown sugar, honey, eggs and vanilla in bowl or mixer. Add mixed flour, baking soda and salt. Stir in walnuts and chocolate mint chips. Drop by teaspoonfuls on greased cookie sheets and bake at 350° f. for 8 to 10 minutes, or until browned and firm

Pineapple Bar Cookies

Here's a dessert for the crowd (100 servings).

INGREDIENTS:

1-1/2	qts honey		1-1/2	qts butter
3	cups eggs, slightly beaten		2-1/4	qts whole wheat flour
3	qts all-purpose flour		2	Tbs baking soda
1	tbs salt		1-1/4	qts canned pineapple, crushed, drained
1-1/4	qts sunflower seeds			
	Cream cheese frosting, prepared (optional)			

METHOD:

Whip honey and butter until creamy. Add eggs and vanilla; continue mixing until blended. Gradually add combined flours, baking soda and salt. Mix well. Fold pineapple and sunflower seeds into batter. Spread batter evenly into each of two 18" x 26" x 1" sheet pans. Bake at 350° F. for 25 to 30 minutes or until lightly browned. Optional - Top each pan with 1 qt frosting. Each pan yields 50 servings.

Oat Bran Cookies

These are low fat, low cholesterol, healthful cookies.

INGREDIENTS:

1/2	cup low-fat margarine		2	cups oat bran
6	Tbs molasses		6	Tbs honey
1-3/4	cup flour		2	egg whites
1	tsp baking soda		1	tsp salt
1	tsp cinnamon		1/2	cup chopped nuts

METHOD:

Mix all ingredients thoroughly. Chill for 2 hours. Form small balls on greased cookie sheets. Flatten balls with bottom of small measuring cup (or mold) dipped in sugar. Bake 10-12 minutes in 350° F. oven.

Honey Date Bars

Luscious, and so simple to make. These bars are moist and chewy and the honey helps keep them that way. This recipe makes about 24 bars.

INGREDIENTS:

2	eggs		3	Tbs margarine
3/4	cup honey		1	cup pitted dates
2/3	cup nuts		3/4	cup sifted flour
3/4	tsp baking powder		1/3	tsp salt

METHOD:

Mix in blender eggs, margarine and honey. When creamy, add dates and chopped nuts. Whirl just enough to mix together. Sift flour, baking powder and salt and add to honey mixture, stirring until combined. Pour into well-greased 8" square pan and bake at 350° F. for 30 minutes or until golden brown. Cut into bars and dip in powdered sugar if desired.

Honey Chocolate Brownies

This recipe makes 16, two inch brownies.

INGREDIENTS:

2	oz unsweetened chocolate		1/3	cup butter or margarine
2	eggs		3/4	cup honey
3/4	cup all-purpose flour		3/4	tsp baking powder
1/2	tsp salt		3/4	cup chopped walnuts

METHOD:

Combine chocolate and butter in small pan and stir over low heat until melted. In large bowl, with electric mixer, beat eggs until thick and fluffy, gradually beat in honey, add chocolate mix. Combine flour, baking soda and salt and add to chocolate mixture, blend. Stir in nuts. Turn into well-greased 8" square pan and bake at 325° F. for 25 to 30 minutes or until toothpick comes out clean. Cool on wire rack. Frost with Honey Cheese Spread .

HONEY CHEESE SPREAD: Beat 2 Tbs honey, 8 oz cream cheese (at room temperature), 1/2 tsp grated fresh orange peel in electric beater bowl until fluffy and well blended. Spread over cooled brownies. Cover tightly and store up to one day. Freeze remaining.

Honey Graham Crackers

Never thought of making your own Graham Crackers? They can be done quick and easy and this is a handy recipe to have in case you need some and don't want to run to the store.

INGREDIENTS:

1/3	cup oil		1/3	cup honey
1/8	cup molasses (2 Tbs)		1	tsp vanilla
2-1/2 to 3	cup whole-wheat pastry flour		1	Tbs dry buttermilk powder
1	tsp baking powder		1/2	tsp baking soda
1/4	tsp salt		1	tsp cinnamon
1/4 to 1/3	cup water			

METHOD:

Mix oil, honey, molasses and vanilla in large bowl. Combine 2-1/2 cups pastry flour with remaining dry ingredients. Add dry mixture to honey mixture, alternating with water. Mix well. If too sticky, add up to 1/2 cup more flour. Form dough into 2 balls. Roll each ball directly onto greased cookie sheet to cover cookie sheet. Preheat oven to 300° F.

FOR CRACKER CRUMBS: Bake 10 minutes, remove from pan and crush into crumbs while still warm. Makes 4 cups.

FOR GRAHAM CRACKERS: Cut into 2-1/2" squares, but do not separate. Prick surface of each cracker with fork. Bake 15 to 25 minutes. Remove to cookie rack and cool.

Orange Marmalade Cookies

These are different. Try them when you want variety and a special tea-time treat. Experiment with other jams, too.

INGREDIENTS:

1/3	cup honey
1/2	cup butter or margarine
1	egg
1/2	tsp vanilla
1	cup flour
1/4	tsp salt
	Orange marmalade

METHOD:

Cream together honey, butter, eggs and vanilla. Stir in flour and salt. Roll into one inch balls. Bake at 375° F. for 5 minutes. Remove from oven and quickly indent centers. Bake 8 minutes longer. Cook and fill with marmalade. Makes 30 cookies.

Crazy Bee Cake

This cake is for persons on special diets. There are no fats, eggs or milk in it.

INGREDIENTS:

3	cups all-purpose flour
1	tsp salt
2	tsp baking soda
6	Tbs cocoa
2	cups honey
1-1/2	cups water
2	Tbs vinegar
1	Tbs vanilla

METHOD:

Sift dry ingredients. In second bowl mix remaining ingredients. Combine and stir lightly. Bake at 350° F. in 13" x 9" pan for about 50 minutes, or until toothpick comes out clean.

Blackberry Crunch

Summer in the Northwest means lots of blackberries. If you don't mind the seeds, leave berries whole, or if you prefer, put berries through a strainer to remove the seeds. Either way this Crunch is good.

INGREDIENTS:

3-1/2 cups blackberries
1   cup honey
1   cup flour
1/2   cup oatmeal
1/2   cup brown sugar
1/2   cup coconut (optional)

METHOD:

Mix blackberries, honey and flour together. Pour into 9" greased pie plate. Sprinkle with oatmeal and brown sugar and coconut if desired. Bake at 350° F. for about 50 minutes or until nicely browned.

Honey Whirl

This recipe was a sweepstakes winner at the Oregon State Fair.

INGREDIENTS:

SWEET DOUGH
1	cup lukewarm water	1/4	cup honey
1	tsp salt	1	pkg (Tbs) dry yeast in
1	egg		1/4 cup warm water
1/4	cup soft shortening	3-1/2 to 4 cups flour	

FILLING
1/3	cup honey	1	cup finely chopped walnuts
1/3	cup butter	1/3	cup cream
2	tsp cinnamon	1-1/2	cups cut raisins

Mix all "Filling" ingredients and cook 1 minute in microwave, cool.

HONEY NUT GLAZE TOPPING
Cook and stir 1/4 cup walnuts in 1 Tbs butter. Add 2 Tbs sugar and 1/4 cup honey. Heat to boiling stirring constantly and cool.

METHOD:

Combine milk, egg, honey, salt an shortening in a large bowl, stir in yeast and add flour in 2 parts, using only enough to make a firm, but not stiff, dough. Knead 5 minutes. Put in bowl and cover, rise once, punch down, rise again. Shape. Put together: Roll dough into 8" x 20" oblong shape, spread with FILLING to 1 inch of edge. Roll up and seal edges. Coil into 10" skillet, bake, after rising double, at 350° F. for 45 to 50 minutes. Spread with HONEY NUT GLAZE.

Honey Corn Kuchen

Speedy and different. Serve for breakfast, lunch or with dinner.

INGREDIENTS:

3/4	cup flour		2-1/2	tsp baking powder
1/2	tsp cinnamon		1/2	tsp nutmeg
1/4	tsp salt		2	cups corn flakes (or bran)
1/2	cup milk		1	egg, well beaten
1/4	cup honey		3	Tbs melted butter or margarine
1/4	cup firmly packed brown sugar		2	Tbs melted butter or margarine

METHOD:

Sift together flour, baking powder and spices. Stir in 1-1/2 cups cornflakes. Combine milk, egg, honey and 3 Tbs melted butter. Add to flour mixture. Mix brown sugar, 2 Tbs melted butter and remaining corn flakes. Pour batter into 8" x 8" x 2" glass baking dish. Top with sugar mixture. Bake in microwave oven 4-1/2 to 5 minutes. Turn dish a quarter every 1-1/2 minutes.

Honey Orange Cake

A potluck specialty. You'll be asked to bring it again, and again.

INGREDIENTS:

1	cup butter or shortening	1	cup honey
4	eggs	1/3	cup orange marmalade
3	cups sifted flour	1	Tbs (3 tsp) baking powder
1/2	tsp soda	1/2	tsp salt
1	cup raisins or diced dates	3/4	cup coarsely chopped walnuts or
	Orange topping		pecans

METHOD:

Cream butter until soft; gradually add honey in a fine stream, beating until light and fluffy. Add eggs and beat well. Stir in marmalade (mixture may curdle a bit). Resift flour with dry ingredients. Combine 1 cup flour mixture with combined raisins and nuts. Beat flour mixture into creamed mixture at low speed until well blended. Stir in fruit and nuts. Pour into greased and floured 9" x 13" pan. Bake at 350° F. (moderate) 35 to 45 minutes, or until cake tests done. Serve warm or cold. Makes 12 to 16 squares.
ORANGE TOPPING: Warm together 1/3 cup honey and 1/3 cup orange juice. Pierce holes in warm cake with fork and spoon syrup onto cake.

Honey Sponge Cake

These dessert squares go well with fresh fruit to complete a meal. Makes about 10 squares.

INGREDIENTS:

5	eggs	3/4	tsp double-acting baking powder
1/4	cup honey	2/3	cup sugar
2	tsp corn oil	3/4	cup sifted flour
	Confectioners' sugar		

METHOD:

Beat eggs until light; add the honey and sugar, beating until thick (about 10 minutes). Sift the flour and baking powder onto the mixture; stir only until smooth. Oil an 8" x 8" brownie pan, and dust with flour. Turn the batter into it. Bake in a preheated 350° F. oven for 35 minutes or until a cake tester comes out clean. Cool on a cake rack 10 minutes, then turn out onto the rack until completely cool. Turn right side up and sprinkle with confectioners' sugar. Cut into 2" squares. Makes about 16 squares.

Honey-Filled Coffee Cake

Called a cake, this delicious honey-filled treat is really a bread. A little extra work, but worth every minute.

INGREDIENTS:

2	pkgs granular yeast	1/4	cup lukewarm water
1/2	cup shortening	2	tsp salt
1/4	cup sugar	1	cup scalded milk
2	eggs, beaten	4-1/2	cups sifted flour

HONEY FILLING

1/2	cup honey	1/2	cup almond paste
1	Tbs orange juice	1-1/2	tsp cinnamon
3/4	cup raisins, cut fine	1/3	cup walnuts, chopped
1	Tbs melted butter		Mix well together

HONEY GLAZE

1/2	cup honey	1/2	cup white sugar
1	Tbs butter		Simmer 5 minutes

METHOD:

Sprinkle yeast over warm water. Let stand 5 minutes until dissolved. Combine shortening, salt and sugar in large bowl. Add scalded milk. Stir until shortening is melted, then cool until lukewarm. Add eggs and yeast; mix well. Add flour, beating thoroughly. Turn onto lightly floured board. Knead until smooth. Place in lightly greased bowl. Cover and let rise until double in bulk. Punch down. Let rest 10 minutes. Divide in 2 parts. Roll out one part into 12" x 16" \rectangle. Brush with melted butter. Spread with half of Honey Filling. Roll like jelly roll and seal edges. Cut into 1" slices. Place cut side, barely touching, in bottom of greased 10" tube pan. Arrange remaining slices in layers, with no slice directly on top of another. Prepare remaining dough on same manner. Cover and let rose until doubled. Bake at 350° F. for 45 to 50 minutes. If browns too fast, lightly place piece of foil on top of pan. When done, pour hot Honey Glaze over hot cake. Decorate with nuts.

Honey Chocolate Cake
with Date Filling

Just reading this recipe can make your mouth water.

INGREDIENTS:

1	cup butter		1-1/2	tsp salt
1-1/2	cup honey		1-1/2	tsp baking soda
3	eggs		1	Tbs baking powder
3	cups sifted flour		1	cup plus 2 Tbs buttermik
1/2	cup cocoa			

METHOD:

Preheat oven to 350° F. sift cocoa, flour and other dry ingredients together. Cream butter and honey, and add eggs. Beat well. Add buttermilk and dry ingredients alternately. Beat well after each addition. Pour into 3 greased and floured 9" cake pans. Bake 35 minutes.

DATE FILLING: Mix in saucepan 1-1/2 cups chopped dates, 1/2 cup orange juice, 1/4 cup honey and 1/2 cup ground filberts. Heat to boiling. Cook until thick. Remove from heat and cool. Spread liberally on first two layers of cake.

HONEY FROSTING: Mix together 1-1/2 cups granulated sugar, 1/4 cup honey, 1/3 cup cold water, 2 egg whites and a dash of salt. Boil in the top of double boiler for 7 minutes, beating constantly until stiff peaks form. Remove from heat and add 1 tsp of vanilla. Beat 2 minutes. Frost top layer and sides.

Mediterranean Cake

A sweet dessert cake, moist, sticky and delicious.

INGREDIENTS:

2	Tbs frozen orange juice concentrate	3/4	cup butter or margarine
3/4	cup honey	3	eggs
1	cup flour	1-1/2	tsp baking powder
1/2	tsp soda	1/2	tsp cinnamon (optional)
1/2	tsp nutmeg	2	Tbs milk
1	Tbs grated orange peel	1	cup chopped walnuts

METHOD:

Cream together butter and honey, add eggs, one at a time, beating well after each addition. Sift together flour, baking powder and spices. Add dry ingredients alternately with milk and 2 Tbs orange juice concentrate. Fold in peel and nuts. Turn into greased and floured 8" square pan. Bake at 350° F. for 30 minutes. Remove from oven and pour honey syrup over cake while it is still hot.

HONEY SYRUP: Mix 1 cup honey and 1/3 cup water. Simmer 5 minutes. Skim and add 1 Tbs frozen orange juice concentrate. Return to heat and boil 2 minutes longer. Cool.

Old Fashioned Jewish Honey Cake

This is a traditional holiday treat, but it is popular everyday fare, too.

INGREDIENTS:

1/2	cup salad oil
2	eggs, beaten
3/4	cup honey
1	cup very strong coffee (Louisiana Style)
1	cup sugar
1	tsp baking powder

1	tsp baking soda
1	tsp cinnamon
1	tsp allspice
3	cups all-purpose flour, sifted
1/2	cup nuts, not chopped too fine (optional)

METHOD:

In a large mixing bowl, add oil to eggs, stirring. Add honey and coffee; then add sugar, gradually, plus all dry ingredients (sifted together), and nuts, mixing thoroughly until a colorful smoothness. Pour into a greased loaf pan and bake in a 325° F. oven for an hour.

Busy Day Honey Cake

This cake whips up in no time at all, and so does the frosting.

INGREDIENTS:

1/2	cup shortening
2	eggs
1	tsp soda
1/2	cup cocoa
2/3	cup milk

1-1/2	cup honey
2	cups flour
1/2	tsp salt
1/4	cup coconut (optional)
	Easy Chocolate Frosting

METHOD:

Cream shortening. Gradually beat in honey until smooth. Add eggs one at a time. Beat well after each. Combine flour, soda, salt, cocoa and coconut. Add dry ingredients alternately with milk to creamed mixture. Pour batter into two greased 9" round cake pans. Bake at 350° F. for 30 minutes or until toothpick comes out clean. Cool in pan for 10 minutes, then remove from pans and finish cooling. Spread Easy Chocolate Frosting between layers and on sides and top of cake.

EASY CHOCOLATE FROSTING: Combine 1/4 cup margarine, 1/4 cup cocoa and 1/4 cup plus 2 Tbs milk over low heat. Bring to boil over low heat. Remove from heat and cool. Gradually add 4 to 5 cups sifted, powdered sugar, beating until mixture is of spreading consistency. Stir in 1 tsp vanilla. Yields enough for one 2 layer cake.

Cherry Coffee Cake

If you appreciate a moist, coffee cake filled with cherries, this one's for you.

INGREDIENTS:

3/4	cup honey		1/2	cup granulated sugar
1/2	cup butter or margarine		1-1/2	tsp baking powder
1	tsp vanilla		1/4	cup milk
4	eggs		3	cups flour
1	can cherry pie filling, or 2 cups pie cherries cooked and thickened with corn starch			

METHOD:

Mix honey, sugar, margarine, milk and vanilla. Add eggs and stir in flour mixed with baking powder. Spread 3/4 of batter on baking sheet. Spread pie filling on top and drop remaining batter, by spoonfuls, spreading a little. Bake at 350° F. for 30 to 40 minutes or until golden brown. When cooled slightly, drizzle with glaze made by mixing 1 cup powdered sugar with 1 to 2 Tbs milk or fruit juice.

Honey Applesauce Cake

A nice, moist variation from banana bread. Any kind of nut meats can put a special crunch in this cake, and you can substitute margarine for the shortening to make it lower in cholesterol.

INGREDIENTS:

2-1/4	cups sifted flour		1/2	cup shortening
1	tsp baking soda		1	cup honey
1	tsp cinnamon		1	egg, well beaten
1/2	tsp cloves		1	cup raisins
1	cup thick, unsweetened applesauce		1	cup broken nut meats

METHOD:

Sift 2 cups flour with soda, salt and spices. Mix remaining flour with raisins and nuts. Cream shortening with honey until fluffy. Add egg and beat thoroughly. Add floured raisins and nuts. Add sifted dry ingredients and applesauce alternately in small amounts, beating well after each addition. Pour into greased pan and bake in moderate oven (350° F.) for 50 to 60 minutes. Makes one (8" x 8") cake.

Frosting

INGREDIENTS:

3	egg whites	1	cup honey
1/4	tsp cream of tartar	5	Tbs cold water

METHOD:

Cook 7 minutes, beat continuously. Garnish with nuts if desired.

"Kiss of the Bee" Chocolate Log

As light as its name implies, and surprisingly easy to put together.

INGREDIENTS:

	Cake			Filling
4	eggs		9	oz cream cheese
1/2	cup honey		1/2	cup honey
1	tsp vanilla		1	tsp vanilla
3/4	cup flour			
1/4	cup sifted cocoa			Frosting
1	tsp baking powder		1/2	cup honey
1/8	tsp salt		2	egg whites
			1/4	tsp cream of tartar
				Pinch of salt
			1	tsp vanilla

METHOD:

Preheat oven to 350° F. Grease a 16" x 12" x 1" jelly roll pan. Line with wax paper, leaving a 2" overhang. Grease and flour paper. Beat eggs, honey and vanilla until very thick and pale, about 5 minutes. Sprinkle with flour, cocoa, baking powder and salt. Fold in. Spread evenly in pan. Bake in preheated oven for 8 to 12 minutes or until center springs back when lightly pressed. Sprinkle top with a little powdered cocoa. Cover with towel and invert to wire rack. Remove pan and peel off paper. Roll up cake and towel together from narrow end. Place seam down on wire rack and cool to room temperature. Unroll cake and spread with filling, leaving an inch border. Roll up tightly and place on plate, seam side down. Frost and garnish with chopped pecans.

FILLING: Beat ingredients until smooth. Top with chopped pecans.

FROSTING: In top of a double boiler, combine honey, egg whites, cream of tartar and salt. Cook over rapidly boiling water, beating until stands in peaks. Remove and add vanilla. Beat until holds deep swirls.

Harvest Lime Spice Cake

Even though it's called "Harvest Cake", this cake can be popular any time of year. It stays moist, too.

INGREDIENTS:

1	cup chopped filberts		1/2	cup margarine
1	cup brown sugar		3/4	cup honey
1	cup cooked or canned pumpkin (mashed)		3	cups all purpose flour
4	tsp baking powder		1/4	tsp baking soda
1	tsp salt		1	tsp cinnamon
1/2	tsp nutmeg		1/4	tsp ground cloves
2	cups milk			

METHOD:

Combine shortening, brown sugar and honey and eggs, beat until creamy. Sift flour, salt and spices together and add to egg mix. Add pumpkin and nuts. Mix lightly. Bake in 2 layer cake pans for 35 minutes at 350°F., or until inserted toothpick comes out clean.

Honey Bread Pudding

Honey Bread Pudding-
Classic as Winnie the Pooh

Each of us, whether a sophisticate or down-home type, each of us has a secret treasury of comforting childhood memories. Memories like the sound of leaves crackling underfoot, the sight of a Flexible Flyer sled leaning against a neighbor's porch or hearing someone quote Winnie the Pooh at a business meeting. Entering a kitchen filled with the aroma of old-fashioned bread pudding can bring back some of the most comforting memories of all.

Our thrifty grandmothers saw bread pudding as a way to kill three birds with one stone. They stretched the food budget, used up over-the-hill bread, and created a tasty dessert—all at the same time.

Stretching the food budget is as much a problem today as it was in our grandmother's day. Which is why this Honey Bread Pudding (page 151) is sure to become one of your family's favorites—not only for dessert, but for breakfast as well. After all, it combines bread, milk and eggs—the foundation for a nutritious breakfast.

And the subtle taste of honey, combined with a hint of orange and rum flavoring, will make this recipe a favorite with guests as well as family.

Another bit of Grandma's wisdom: Because honey absorbs and retains moisture readily, baked goods will not dry out or become stale as quickly as products made with granulated sugar. Store honey at room temperature. If it crystallizes, just remove lid and place jar in warm water until crystal dissolves. Or microcook 1 cup of honey in a microwave-safe container at HIGH for 2 to 3 minutes, or until crystals dissolve; stir every 30 seconds.

Honey Cheesecake

Cheesecake is best when aged 2 to 3 days. It will be difficult to keep this one so long.

INGREDIENTS:

Filling
3/4	cup honey
4	eggs
24	oz cream cheese
2	tsp vanilla
2	tsp lemon juice

Topping
2	cups sour cream
1/4	cup honey

Crust
3	cups graham cracker crumbs (look under "Specialties" for Graham Cracker recipe)
1/2	cup butter
3	Tbs honey

METHOD:

Combine crust ingredients and press into a springform pan. Chill. Whip honey and 2 egg whites until fluffy. Set aside. Cream softened cream cheese until light. Add remaining eggs, vanilla, lemon juice and honey mixture, in this order, whipping thoroughly. Pour filling into prepared crust. Bake 45 minutes at 350° F. Remove from oven and refrigerate cake for 10 minutes. Increase oven temperature to 400° F. Prepare topping by combining sour cream and honey. Pour topping over cake and return to 400° F. oven for 5 minutes. Cool 45 to 60 minutes, then refrigerate cake.

Honey Rum Fruit Topper

Rub salt on pineapple, and then rinse carefully before serving. This removes the acid that makes some people's mouths sore.

INGREDIENTS:

1/2   cup honey
3 to 4 tsp rum (one tsp rum flavoring can be substituted)
1   fresh pineapple
2   oranges, peeled and sliced
1   cup grapes

METHOD:

Stir honey and rum together until well blended; set aside. Cut pineapple in half lengthwise including green top. Carefully carve fruit from center leaving shell intact. Slice pineapple pieces; toss with remaining fruit and honey mixture. Marinate 1 hour. Arrange in pineapple shells. Makes 4 servings. Preparation Time: About 30 minutes.

Honey Lemon Pie

For a special lemon pie, try making it with honey instead of sugar. If you use a large size pie tin, increase the egg yolks to four and add extra lemon juice (for a nice lemony flavor).

INGREDIENTS:

3/4	cup light honey
1/2	cup cornstarch
1-1/2	cups water
3	eggs yolks
1/4	cup lemon juice
1	Tbs grated lemon rind
3	Tbs margarine

METHOD:

Mix honey and cornstarch in saucepan. Gradually stir in water. Cook over medium heat, stirring constantly, until mixture thickens and boils. Boil 1 minute. Slowly stir in at least half the hot mixture into egg yolks. Then blend into hot mixture in saucepan. Boil 1 minute longer. stirring constantly. Remove from heat. Continue stirring until smooth. Blend in margarine, lemon juice and rind. Pour into baked pie shell. Cover with meringue and bake. Serve when cool.

Pie Crust

INGREDIENTS:

1	cup sifted whole wheat flour or all purpose
3/4	tsp honey
1/8	tsp salt
1	tsp baking powder
5	tbs butter or margarine
2-3	tbs ice-cold water

METHOD:

Cut butter and honey into dry ingredients with pastry blender or two forks. Sprinkle ice water, a tsp at a time, over mixture, blending lightly with each addition. Add only enough water to hold pastry together. Shape into a ball and roll to 10" circles. Transfer to pie tins, fill, and flute edges.

Pie Meringue

INGREDIENTS:

3   egg whites
1/4   tsp cream of tartar
6   tbs light honey
1/2   tsp lemon juice

METHOD:

Heat oven to 400° F. Beat egg whites with cream of tartar until stiff. Gradually beat in honey, then lemon juice. Pile meringue onto hot pie filling, being careful to seal meringue onto edge of crust to prevent shrinking or weeping. Swirl or pull up points for decorative top. Bake 5 to 8 minutes until delicately browned.

Pumpkin Pie

This recipe makes two 9 inch pies.

INGREDIENTS:

4	eggs, slightly beaten (can be 6 whites)
3/4	cup honey
2	tsp cinnamon or nutmeg
1/2	tsp ground cloves (optional)

1	can (26 oz) pumpkin
1	tsp salt
1	tsp ground ginger
2	cans evaporated milk or 3-1/4 cup milk

METHOD:

Preheat oven to 425° F. Combine filling ingredients in order given; divide evenly into pie shells. Bake 15 minutes. Reduce oven temperature to 350° F. and bake an additional 45 minutes, or until centers of pie are solid. Top with whipping cream or non-fat whipped milk.

Frosty Cranberry Pie

In the fall when cranberries are plentiful, select bags of firm berries and freeze right in the bag. Then you can enjoy elegant desserts with cranberries year-round.

INGREDIENTS:

1-1/2	cups fine vanilla or lemon wafer crumbs
6	Tbs butter or margarine, melted
1	cup whipping cream
1	tsp vanilla
1	pkg (8 oz) cream cheese
1/4	cup honey
1	can (1 Lb.) whole cranberry sauce
	Additional whipped cream for garnish

METHOD:

Combine cookie crumbs and butter. Press firmly over bottom and sides of 9" pie pan. Chill. Whip cream with vanilla until thickened but not too stiff. With same beaters, soften cream cheese; gradually add honey in a fine stream, beating until smooth. Fold whipped cream into cheese mixture. Set aside a few berries from sauce to use as garnish. Fold remaining cranberry sauce into whipped mixture. Spoon into crust. Cover with plastic film and freeze until firm. Remove from freezer 10 minutes before serving. If desired, top with honey sweetened whipped cream. Garnish with reserved cranberries. Makes 8 to 10 rich servings.

Blueberry Honey Pie

Use either domestic blueberries or wild huckleberries. If you are lucky enough to find wild red huckleberries, this will be the best pie you ever ate.

INGREDIENTS:

6	cups blueberries
3/4	cup honey
1/4	tsp salt
4	Tbs cornstarch
1/4	cup water
2	tsp lemon juice
2	tsp margarine or butter

METHOD:

Mix 5 cups blueberries, honey and salt. Add water to cornstarch and blend into blueberries. In saucepan, cook over medium heat until bubbly and clean, about 2 minutes. Stir in lemon juice, margarine and remaining cup of blueberries. Cool slightly and pour into baked 9" pie shell. Chill. Serve with honey Whipped Cream.

Crepes

INGREDIENTS:

3   whole eggs plus 1 yolk
1/3   cup oil
       About 2-1/2 cups milk

1-1/2 cups whole wheat pastry flour
3/4   tsp brewer's yeast

METHOD:

Combine flour, whole eggs, egg yolk. oil, brewer's yeast and 3/4 cup milk in medium bowl. Beat until smooth. Add additional milk to give the batter consistency of light cream. Cover and refrigerate 30 minutes. When ready to cook, heat medium-size pan over medium heat. Dip paper towel in oil and wipe pan. Ladle about 1/4 cup batter into pan. Tilt pan to cover bottom with thin coat of batter. When crepe is dry on top, turn. Place on heat-proof platter in "low" oven until ready.

Fiesta Fruit Dressing

A year round favorite.

INGREDIENTS:

1 cup mayonnaise (not salad dressing)
1/4 cup honey
1 Tbs grated orange peel
1 Tbs fresh orange juice

METHOD:

Combine all ingredients and chill. Serve over well drained chilled fruits. Makes about 1-1/4 cup.

Nippy Nectar Dressing

Use this dressing for any type of fruit salad.

INGREDIENTS:

1	3 oz pkg cream cheese
1	Tbs honey
1	tsp grated lemon peel
1	Tbs lemon juice
1/2	tsp salt
1/2	cup salad oil

METHOD:

Soften cream cheese, blend with remaining ingredients except oil. Add oil 1 Tbs at a time, beating well after each addition. Chill. Beat again before serving over fruit salad.

Judy's Honey Dressing

Another variation of the popular honey-mustard dressing that is growing in popularity.

INGREDIENTS:

1/4 to 1/3 cup vinegar
1/2   cup honey (mildly flavored)
2   Tbs lemon juice
1/8   tsp onion salt
1   tsp celery seed
1/8   tsp dry mustard

METHOD:

Mix ingredients in a blender (or with a rotary beater). Slowly add 1 cup salad oil, blending or beating constantly. Chill before serving on fruit or vegetable salads.

Baked Prune Pudding

If you are fortunate enough to have a prune tree, this will be one of your favorite recipes. If you have to buy prunes at the store, six or seven will make a cup of chopped pulp, or you can use canned prunes.

INGREDIENTS:

1/4	cup cracker crumbs (4 crackers)
3/4	tsp baking powder
1/2	cup honey
1	cup seeded cooked prunes, drained and chopped
1	tsp vanilla

1/4	cup evaporated milk
1/4	cup water
1	Tbs melted butter
1	tsp salt
1/4	cup chopped walnuts or pecans

METHOD:

Mix cracker crumbs thoroughly with the baking powder; then combine with all ingredients thoroughly, and turn into a buttered glass loaf pan (8-12" x 4-1/2" x 1-3/4"). Bake in a moderate oven (350° F.) for 30 minutes. Serve hot with milk or cream. 5 servings

Ambrosia with Honey Cream Dressing

A pretty dessert that you can show off right at the table in an elegant glass bowl. If you want to skip the whipping cream, you can substitute yogurt.

INGREDIENTS:

1/4	cup honey
2	Tbs lime juice
2	medium oranges, peeled and sliced
2	bananas, peeled and sliced
1	<u>each</u> red and green apple, cored and cubed
1	cup shredded coconut
	Honey Lime Cream Dressing

METHOD:

Combine honey and lime juice; toss with fruit. Layer fruit alternately with coconut in serving bowl. Top with Honey Lime Cream Dressing. Makes 4 servings.

HONEY LIME CREAM DRESSING: Beat 1/2 cup whipping cream until fluffy. Drizzle in 2 Tbs honey and beat until stiff. Fold in 1 tsp grated lime peel. Makes 1 cup. Preparation Time: Less than 30 minutes.

Date Torte

A special dessert that your guests will rave about. This recipe makes 18 to 24 servings.

INGREDIENTS:

2	cups sifted dry bread crumbs		1/2	cup sifted all-purpose flour
1	tsp baking powder		4	eggs, separated
2	cups honey		2	cups chopped, pitted dates
1	cup chopped walnuts		2	tsp vanilla extract
	Whipped cream			Dash salt

METHOD:

Preheat oven to 375° F. Grease a cake pan (13" x 9" x 2"). Sift together the bread crumbs, flour, salt and baking powder. Set aside. Beat the egg yolks lightly. Add the honey and mix thoroughly. Add dates, walnuts, vanilla and sifted dry ingredients. Mix well. Beat the egg whites until stiff peaks are formed. Fold gently into the batter. Pour into the prepared pan. Bake for 25 to 30 minutes, until the cake rebounds to the touch when pressed gently in the center. Remove the cake from the oven, cut into squares, and serve hot with whipped cream.

Honey Sabayon

A quick dessert for company, or special occasion. The microwave makes it easy.

INGREDIENTS:

1-1/2 cups half-and-half	1/4 cup honey
1 Tbs cornstarch	2 eggs, beaten
1 tsp vanilla	1/2 tsp grated orange peel
Strawberry Sauce	Whole, fresh strawberries

METHOD:

Combine half-and-half, honey and cornstarch in microwave-safe one quart container. Micro cook at HIGH 100%) 4 to 5 minutes stirring halfway through cooking time. Blend small amount of hot liquid with eggs; return to hot mixture and stir well. Micro cook at HIGH 30 to 60 seconds or until mixture comes to boil and thickens; stir after 30 seconds. Stir in vanilla and peel. Cool, stirring occasionally. Pour into serving dishes; decorate with Strawberry Sauce. Garnish with sliced strawberry if desired. Makes 4 servings.

STRAWBERRY SAUCE: Puree one 10 ounce box frozen sliced strawberries, thawed; blend in 2 to 3 tsps cornstarch. Micro cook at HIGH 3 to 5 minutes or until thickened, stirring every minute. Makes about 1 1/4 cups.

TIP: Add 2 Tbs brandy or cream sherry for a festive touch.

Preparation Time: Less than 30 minutes.

Lemon Bread Pudding

Another version of the ever-popular bread pudding.

INGREDIENTS:

1/4	cup margarine	2	cups bread cubes
2	tsp grated lemon peel	2	Tbs lemon juice
1	cup milk	3	eggs
1/2 to 1/4 cup honey (to taste)		1/2	cup raisins

METHOD:

Melt butter and mix with lemon and lemon peel. Coat bread crumbs with mixture, tossing lightly In bowl, beat milk, honey and egg and pour over bread cubes. Sprinkle raisins over top. Place dish in pan of water and bake in 325° F. oven for 50 minutes, or until center firms.

Honey Bread Pudding

Remember bread pudding? It's on the dessert tray at the fanciest restaurants again.

INGREDIENTS:

8	cups day-old egg bread, cubed	3	cups milk
1	cup half-and half	6	eggs, beaten
1/2	cup honey	1	Tbs grated orange peel
1	tsp <u>each</u> vanilla and ground cinnamon		Honey Cream Sauce

METHOD:

Arrange bread in bottom of lightly greased shallow two-quart baking dish. Beat remaining ingredients until well blended; pour over bread cubes in baking dish and let stand 1 hour or until liquid is absorbed by bread. Bake at 375° F. 45 to 50 minutes or until knife inserted near center comes out clean. Makes 8 to 12 servings. Recipe can be halved.

HONEY CREAM SAUCE: Beat 1 cup whipping cream until fluffy; add 1/4 cup honey slowly and beat until stiff. Fold in 1 Tbs rum (one-half tsp rum extract can be substituted). Makes about 2 cups.

Honey Rhubarb Compote

This compote is a Norwegian favorite. It is simple to make and adds a nice variety to dessert time.

INGREDIENTS:

1 cup water	1/2 tsp vanilla
1/2 to 3/4 cup honey	2 Tbs cornstarch
4 cups (1 1/2 lb.) rhubarb washed, trimmed and cut in 1/2 inch pieces (frozen rhubarb may be substituted)	3 Tbs cold water
	Whipped cream

METHOD:

Dissolve honey in 2-quart non-aluminum saucepan ; bring to boil. Add rhubarb; reduce heat and simmer, uncovered, 15 to 25 minutes or until rhubarb is tender but still in distinct pieces. Stir in vanilla. Combine cornstarch with 3 Tbs water; mix well. Gradually stir cornstarch mixture into cooked rhubarb; cook and stir until mixture comes to boil. Simmer 3 to 5 minutes or until mixture thickens. Pour into serving bowl and refrigerate until cold. Serve with whipped cream. Makes about 6 servings.

WHIPPED CREAM: Beat 1 cup whipping cream until mixture thickens; gradually add 3 Tbs honey and beat until soft peaks form. Fold in 1 tsp vanilla. makes about 2 cups.

Honey Rice Pudding

Rice pudding has been a staple since grandma's time. It's good and it's healthy. To reduce the calories use low-fat milk.

INGREDIENTS:

1-1/2	cups water
1/4	tsp salt
2	cups milk, divided
1	egg, beaten
1/4	cup honey

1	Tbs butter or margarine
1-1/4	cups pre-cooked rice
1/2	cup golden raisins
4	tsps cornstarch
1	tsp <u>each</u> vanilla and grated orange peel

METHOD:

Bring water, butter and salt to boil in heavy saucepan; stir in rice. Cover and remove from heat; Let stand 5 minutes. Stir in 1-1/2 cups milk a nd raisins. Cook over medium heat about 15 to 20 minutes or until thickened; stir constantly. Mix remaining milk, egg and cornstarch; slowly stir into rice mixture. Cook 2 minutes. Stir in honey, vanilla and orange peel. Cool to warm, stirring occasionally. Serve warm. Makes 6 servings.

Spiced Apple Topping

A pancake breakfast for about 100 persons? Give them a special treat by putting about 1/4 cup of this topping over pancakes or French toast.

INGREDIENTS:

1	qt honey	1/2	cup butter
1	cup cornstarch	2	Tbs ground cinnamon
1	Tbs ground nutmeg	3	qts apple juice
1	gal apples, cored, thinly sliced		Salt (optional)

METHOD:

Mix honey and butter; dissolve cornstarch, cinnamon and nutmeg in apple juice. Add to honey mixture. Cook and stir until thickened and clear. Add apples and return to simmer. Add salt if desired, Remove from heat.

Honey-Apple Dessert Sauce

Spoon Honey-Apple Desert sauce over ice cream, pound cake, angel food or gingerbread. Mmm - good!

INGREDIENTS:

1/2	cup sliced almonds
1/4	cup butter or margarine, divided
2	cups pared and sliced Golden Delicious apples
1/2	cup honey
1/4	cup packed brown sugar
2	Tbs dark rum
3 to 4	tsp cornstarch

METHOD:

In large skillet over medium heat, brown almonds in 2 tsp butter; stir frequently. Do not let butter burn. With slotted spoon remove almonds; set aside. Add remaining butter to skillet. Cook and stir apple slices in butter 2 to 3 minutes or until tender. Add honey and brown sugar. Combine rum and cornstarch; stir into apple mixture. Bring to boil. Cook and stir over medium heat 1 minute or until sauce thickens. Stir in almonds. Makes 2 1/2 cups. Prepare Time: Less than 30 minutes.

Cottage Cheese Brunch Blintzes

Serve for brunch or late dinners. You can experiment with different honey jams as fillings replacing the orange juice as well as using for topping with sour cream. If you use jam filling, add a little lemon juice to the filling mix.

INGREDIENTS:

2	cups cottage cheese
1	egg white (left from crepe recipe below)
2	Tbs orange juice concentrate
1/4	tsp salt
1/2	batch crepes (see page 142)
	Sour cream and honey-sweetened jam

2	whole eggs
3	Tbs honey
1/2	tsp cinnamon (optional)
1/3	cup currants
3	Tbs slivered almonds

METHOD:

Heat oven to 425° F. Combine cottage cheese, eggs, honey, orange juice, cinnamon, salt and currants. Place 2 to 3 Tbs filling in center of each crepe. Fold into a pocket by first folding up the bottom flap, then the side flaps. Tuck in upper flap and place blintz on lightly greased, oven-proof serving platter. Brush tops lightly with melted butter and sprinkle with slivered almonds. Bake 15 minutes or until lightly toasted. Decorate tops with sour cream and jam before serving.

Honey Caramel Sauce

Serve warm over ice cream, custard or pudding.

INGREDIENTS:

1-1/2   cups honey
1/2   cup heavy cream
1   Tbs butter or margarine
1   tsp vanilla
1/8   tsp salt

METHOD:

Combine honey and cream in heavy saucepan; cook and stir over medium-high heat until mixture reaches 238° F. Stir in butter, vanilla and salt. Cool. Makes 1 3/4 cups. Preparation Time: Less than 30 minutes.

Frozen Honey Yogurt

Frozen desserts made with honey are delectable.

INGREDIENTS:

2	cups milk
3/4	cup honey
2	beaten eggs
1	pint plain yogurt
1	Tbs vanilla
	Dash salt

METHOD:

Heat milk but do not boil; stir in honey and salt. Pour small amount of hot liquid into eggs; return to milk mixture. Cook and stir over medium-low heat 5 minutes. Cool thoroughly. Stir in yogurt and vanilla. Refrigerate until cold. Turn into 13" x 9" x 2" metal pan. Freeze until firm; stir every 20 to 30 minutes. Makes 1 quart.

Strawberry Honey Ice Cream

It doesn't seem like summer without homemade ice cream. This recipe is equally good with other berries. Try it with blueberries, raspberries or strained blackberry pulp (to remove seeds). For a lighter version substitute 1% milk for all or part of the whipping cream.

INGREDIENTS:

6	large eggs, beaten
1/2	tsp salt
2	cups honey
4	cups half & half
2	cups whipping cream
2	Tbs vanilla
2-1/2 to 3 cups mashed sliced fresh strawberries	

Handwritten notes:
3 eggs
1/4 tsp salt
1 c. honey
2 c. half & half
1 c. whipping cream
1 Tbsp Vanilla
+ fruit

ice cream maker holds 5¾ cups

METHOD:

Beat eggs and salt. Slowly add honey. Or mix in Blender. Add 2 cups half & half. Cook 20 minutes in double boiler over water. Stir frequently. Remove from heat. Add remaining 2 cups half & half, whipping cream and vanilla. Stir in strawberries. Fill ice cream container 3/4 full and chill in the refrigerator. Stir, then freeze according to the ice cream freezer directions. Upon removal of paddle, restir strawberries through ice cream. Pack ice/salt mixture or put in freezer for 4 hours. During strawberry season serve topped with fresh strawberry sauce.

Chocolate Honey Ice Cream

For a lighter version, substitute 1% milk for all or part of the cream. The texture won't be as creamy, but the taste is still delicious.

INGREDIENTS:

2	ounces baking chocolate or 1/2 cup plus 1 Tbs cocoa and carob powder
1-1/2	Tbs butter
2	cups mild honey
5	large eggs, beaten
1/2	tsp salt
4	cups half and half
4	cups whipping cream
1-1/2	Tbs vanilla

METHOD:

Melt chocolate in double boiler. Slowly add honey, then beaten eggs, salt and 2 cups half and half. Cook 20 minutes over water stirring enough to keep mixture smooth. Remove from heat. Add remaining 2 cups half and half, whipping cream and vanilla. Fill ice cream container 3/4 full. Chill in refrigerator. Freeze according to ice cream freezer directions. Pack in ice/salt mixture or put in containers to ripen in freezer 4 hours.

Hot Papaya Sundae

During the lull between winter and summer fruits, tropicals are a good choice. Papayas are ripe when they are golden and give slightly when pressed.

INGREDIENTS:

1	Tbs margarine, melted
1/2	tsp shaved lime peel
1/4	cup lime juice
1/3	cup rum or water
3	Tbs honey
2	medium firm ripe papayas
	Vanilla ice cream

METHOD:

In a small baking dish or pie tin, combine margarine, lime peel and juice, rum and honey. Cut papayas in half lengthwise and remove black seeds. Place papayas cut side down in pan. Bake in 375° F. oven until papayas are hot and sauce begins to boil (about 15 minutes). Remove papayas and place cut side up on dessert plates. Cool slightly and fill halves with scoop of ice cream. Pour pan juices into pitcher and offer as topping. Serves four.

Crushed Pineapple Ice Cream

This recipe is also good, even better, if you add a cup of crushed banana. For lighter version (less calories) substitute 4 cups of 1% milk for whipping cream.

INGREDIENTS:

5	large eggs
2	cups mild honey
2	cups half & half
4	cups whipping cream
1	Tbs vanilla
2	cans (15-1/2 oz.) crushed pineapple (approx. 3-1/4 cup)

METHOD:

Beat eggs. Gradually add honey, salt and half & half. May be mixed in blender. Cook 20 minutes in double boiler over water. Stir occasionally. Remove from heat. Cool slightly, then add whipping cream, vanilla and crushed pineapple. Fill ice cream container 2/3 to 3/4 full. Add regular milk if needed. Chill in refrigerator until cold. Freeze according to ice cream freezer directions. When ice cream is made, either pack in ice salt mixture or ripen in freezer approximately 4 hours.

Honey Berry Sauce for Ice Cream

Keep this delicious topping in the refrigerator for a quick and easy dessert treat.

INGREDIENTS:

1	cup <u>each</u> frozen blackberries, blueberries, and raspberries
3/4	cup cranberry juice
1/4	cup honey
1-1/2	tsps grated orange peel

METHOD:

Combine berries, fresh or frozen. Drain and reserve 1/2 cup liquid. Combine cranberry juice, reserved liquid and honey; bring to boil over high heat. Reduce heat to medium, simmer about 10 minutes, or until mixture is reduced to 1 cup. Remove from heat; stir in orange peel. Cool; pour over berries, chill until serving time; spoon over ice cream or fruit sherbet. Makes 3 cups. Refrigerate covered up to one week.

Fresh Fruit Pizza

INGREDIENTS:

1	batch raised roll dough (see below)
12	oz cream cheese
1/3	cup honey
1/2	cup apricot jam
2	Tbs honey
	Sliced fresh fruit (almost any kind)

METHOD:

Roll dough evenly on a 14" pizza pan. Let rise and bake at 375° F. for 12 minutes. Cool on wire rack. Whip cream cheese and honey until smooth and creamy. Spread on crust. Cover with fruit slices. Melt jam and honey on top of fruit. chill before serving.

Royalty Chocolate Sauce

Serve over ice cream, cake squares, or chilled canned pears. "It's worth the calories."

INGREDIENTS:

2	squares unsweetened chocolate
1/4	cup water
1/2	cup honey
1/4	tsp salt
3	tbs butter or margarine
1/2	tsp vanilla or rum or brandy extract

METHOD:

Combine chocolate, water, honey and salt in small saucepan. Stir over low heat until chocolate is melted. Increase heat to medium and cook until sauce is smooth and slightly thickened. Remove from heat. Stir in butter and vanilla. Serve warm or cold over ice cream, cake squares or chilled canned pears. Makes about 1 cup.

HOLIDAY HINT: Stir 1/3 cup glacè cherries into sauce.

Drinks with Honey

Honey Punch

This recipe makes about 24 half-cup servings. Adding champagne for festive occasions is optional.

INGREDIENTS:

1	quart boiling water
1	tea bag
5	cloves (whole)
1	cup orange juice
1	can (12 oz) limeade
1/2	cup lemon juice
1/2	cup honey
1	quart cold water

METHOD:

Pour boiling water over tea bag and cloves. Cover and let steep for 5 minutes, then strain. Blend honey into tea while warm, combine tea mixture with other ingredients and pour over cracked ice to chill. Garnish with orange slices and mint leaves. Makes about 24 half-cup servings.

Fruit Honey-Yogurt Nog

A healthy drink that makes four or five servings. Use non-fat yogurt if you are counting calories or on a diet.

INGREDIENTS:

1	carton (8 oz or 1 cup) plain or flavored yogurt
1	cup water
1	egg
8 to 12	ice cubes

1	can (6 oz) frozen fruit juice concentrate (any flavor)
1/3	cup honey
1-1/2	tsp vanilla
	Orange slices (optional)

METHOD:

In blender container, place yogurt, water, juice concentrate, honey, egg and vanilla. Cover and blend on high speed about 1 minute or until smooth. Through hole in lid of blender, or with the lid slightly ajar, add ice cubes, one at a time, while blending at high speed; blend until smooth. Pour into tall glasses; garnish each serving with as orange slice, if desired. Makes 4 to 5 servings.

Peach Frosty

Liquify peaches in blender first so you will only have to wash it once.

INGREDIENTS:

1-1/2   cup peach nectar
       Juice of 2 lemons
1   Tbs honey
       Ice cream or crushed ice

METHOD:

Put crushed ice in the blender, add the other ingredients. Beat until well mixed and frothy. Pour into chilled goblets and serve.

Tea Punch

This punch os a nice party drink and looks great in the punchbowl.

INGREDIENTS:

3	cups orange juice
3	cups grapefruit juice
2	tsp instant tea
1/2	cup honey
2	cups warm water
1	pint ginger ale

METHOD:

Blend honey into water. (I often use herb tea rather than instant, and blend honey into the tea.) Mix juices and tea and pour over ice in a punch bowl. Add ginger ale and stir a bit.

Honey-ade Milk Shake

A quick pick-you-up drink for a warm afternoon. Honey makes it good.

INGREDIENTS:

1/3	cup mild honey
1	can (6 oz) frozen lemonade or frozen orange juice
4	scoops vanilla ice cream
3	cups cold milk

METHOD:

Combine honey, lemonade and ice cream. Add milk. Shake, blend or beat with rotary beater to mix well. Serve immediately. Makes 1 quart or 4 servings.

Honey Granola-Delicious, High Energy Snack

When the kids come in hungry, when you've got the nervous nibbles or when you're looking for something to spark up a simple dessert, nothing beats Honey Granola

As a snack food, it satisfies the sweet tooth with its subtle flavor of honey combined with butter and cinnamon. Its crisp texture pleases the palate that demands something to crunch on. And the nutrition-conscious can enjoy it with a clear conscience because the rolled oats, chopped nuts and raisins provide generous amounts of vitamins, minerals and fiber, as well as a modicum of protein.

Honey Granola also adds a unique flavor and crunchy texture when sprinkled on canned or fresh fruit.

Keep a supply on hand to take along to the game, on weekend drives or to munch on while watching your favorite movie or TV program.

Remember, at 21 calories per teaspoon, honey is about one and one-half times as sweet as sugar. In recipes calling for sugar, honey can be substituted for up to one-half the sugar, but be sure to reduce the amount of liquid in the recipe about 1/2 for each cup of honey used. For baked goods, add about 1/2-teaspoon baking soda for each cup of honey used. Honey adds a golden brown color to baked goods. When substituting honey for sugar, reduce baking temperature by 25° F. for even browning.

Granola

Nutritious and delicious. A great after-school treat and one that is healthy.

INGREDIENTS:

6	cups quick rolled oats	1	cup shredded coconuts
1	cup wheat germ	1/2	cup sunflower seeds
3/4	cup halves cashews	1/2	cup cooking oil
1/2	cup honey	1 to 3	cups water
1-1/2	tsp vanilla	1	cup raisins
1	cup chopped dry apricots	1	cup chopped dates

METHOD:

In a large bowl, combine oats, coconut, wheat germ, sunflower seeds and cashews. Mix together oil, honey, water, salt and vanilla; stir until coated. Bake at 350° F. for 30 minutes, stirring frequently. Cool, and add fruit. Store in airtight container until ready for use. Makes 11 cups (500 calories per cup).

Zaps

A healthy sweet treat. If mix is sticky you used too much water, shake balls in bag with powdered sugar.

INGREDIENTS:

Mix together thoroughly:
1	cup peanut butter
1	cup almond butter
1	Cup honey
1	Tbs vanilla

Blend and pour over mixture:
1-1/3	cup coconut
1/2	cup sunflower seeds meal
1/2	cup non-instant powdered milk
1	cup wheatgerm
1/2	cup oatbran
1/2	cup carob powder
	Water

METHOD:

blend first 4 ingredients. Slowly add remaining ingredients. Add only enough water to make the right consistency to form into balls. Chill to blend flavors and serve.

Popcorn Crunch

INGREDIENTS:

1/2	cup melted butter
1/2	cup honey
3	quarts popped popcorn
1	cup nuts

METHOD:

Blend butter and honey. Heat until well blended. Pour over popcorn-nut mixture. Mix well. Spread over cookie sheet in this layer. Bake in preheated 300° F. oven for 10 minutes.

Honey Snack Drops

Elegant cookies that are as good as they look.

INGREDIENTS:

1	cup chopped filberts		1	cup honey
2	Tbs sugar		1/2	cup water
1	cup grated coconut		1	slightly beaten egg
1/4	tsp salt		1/2	cup flour
1/2	tsp ground ginger		1/2	tsp baking powder
1/4	cup chopped dates		1/2	cup white raisins

METHOD:

Toast filberts in 325° F. oven for 5 minutes. Rub in rough towel to remove skins. Chop. In saucepan combine honey, sugar and water. Cook, stirring constantly until dissolved. Add coconut and boil for about 20 minutes or until mix is caramel colored and thickened. (Stir to prevent burning). Cool, mix flour, salt, baking powder and ginger and add to honey mix. Add dates, raisins and chopped filberts. Beat in egg until well blended. Drop by teaspoonfuls onto greased cookie sheet. Bake at 300° F. for 15 minutes, or until nicely browned.

Honey Delights

Another healthy treat that's good any time of year.

INGREDIENTS:

1	cup honey
1/2	cup butter or margarine
1	cup cup cashews
1-1/2	cup pecans
1-3/4	cup coconut

METHOD:

Cook butter and honey for 10 minutes, or to hard boil stage. Pour over cashews that have been slightly chopped. Cool until able to handle, and roll into small balls. Roll balls in coconut and top each with pecan for decoration.

Fruit Leather

Heating the fruit and honey to almost boiling is necessary to retain color and prevent darkening of fresh peaches, pears, apples, apricots, cherries or nectarines. No cooking is required for fresh plums, raspberries, blackberries, cranberries, strawberries or boysenberries.

INGREDIENTS:

4	cups fruit purèe
1/4	cup mild flavored honey

METHOD:

Purèe fruit in a blender and blend together with honey. Pour into saucepan and heat to almost boiling. Cool. Pour onto trays or baking sheets lined with plastic wrap. Each layer or fruit purèe should be 1/4" thick or less. Place trays in a dehydrator at 140° F. or in the oven at 150° F. for 4 to 6 hours, or outside in the sun for 1 to 2 days. Leather is done when "leather-like" and pliable. Remove the leather from the trays while it is still warm and roll it up. Wrap it in plastic sheet. Makes four to five 8" x 10" sheets.

Oven Caramel Corn

Add this recipe to your favorite snack foods. It's better and fresher when you make it at home.

INGREDIENTS:

3-3/4   quarts popped corn
1   cup honey
1/2   cup margarine
1/2   tsp salt
1/2   tsp baking soda

METHOD:

Heat oven to 200° F. Divide popped corn on two ungreased baking sheets. Heat honey, margarine and salt; boil 5 minutes or until soft ball stage (326° F.). Remove from heat and stir in soda until foamy. Pour over popped corn to coat. Bake one hour, stirring every 15 minutes.

Tortilla Crisps with Honey Dip

This recipe comes from Mexico. It is a little different, but if you try it, you'll like it.

INGREDIENTS:

1/2	cup honey
2	Tbs butter or margarine
1	small (about 2-in.) cinnamon stick
1	piece (1 1/2 x 1/2-in.) orange peel
6	(about 6-in. each) flour or corn tortillas, cut in six wedges
	Vegetable oil

METHOD:

Combine honey, butter, cinnamon stick and orange peel. Cook over low heat at least 10 minutes. Remove cinnamon stick and peel before serving. Deep fry tortilla, smooth-side up, at 350° F. about 30 seconds. Turn and deep-fry 30 seconds longer or until golden brown. Tortilla should puff as soon as they are put in hot oil. Remove from oil to paper towel-lined tray. Serve crisp tortilla with honey dip or spoon dip over chips. Makes 6 servings.

OVEN METHOD: Brush both sides of whole tortilla with vegetable oil. Cut into wedges before baking, if desired. Place on baking sheet and bake at 325° F. about 12 minutes or until crisp and browned but not hard.

Old Fashioned Fudge

When perfect, fudge is creamy, but not soft; firm , but not too hard, and utterly delicious! Makes about 32 squares.

INGREDIENTS:

1	cup honey		2/3	cups milk
2	oz unsweetened chocolate or 1/2 cup cocoa		2	Tbs corn syrup
1/4	tsp salt		2	Tbs butter or margarine
1	tsp vanilla		1/2	cup coarsely chopped nuts

METHOD:

Butter 9" x 5" pan. In 2 quart saucepan mix honey, milk, chocolate, corn syrup and salt. Cook over medium heat, stirring constantly until chocolate is melted and honey dissolved. Continue cooking, stirring frequently until mix reaches 236° F. on candy thermometer or soft ball stage. Remove from heat ; add butter, cool to 120° F. without stirring (bottom of pan will be luke warm). Add vanilla and beat vigorously until candy is thick and loses its gloss. (will hold shape when dropped from spoon). Add nuts quickly and spread evenly in pan. When firm cut into squares.

Huckleberry Honey Jells

INGREDIENTS:

3/4	cup huckleberries, pureed
1/4	cup water
1	box Sure-Jell fruit pectin
1/2	tsp soda
1	cup sugar
1	cup honey
1	cup chopped walnuts (optional)

METHOD:

Measure 3/4 cup huckleberry puree in one cup measure, add water to make 1 cup. Pour into a 2 quart saucepan, add fruit pectin and soda. Stir well. (Mixture will foam slightly.) In another 3 quart saucepan, combine the honey and sugar. Place both saucepans over high heat, and cook both mixtures, stirring alternately, until foam has thinned from fruit mixture and the sugar mixture is boiling rapidly, about 5 minutes. Slowly pour the fruit mixture into the sugar mixture, stirring constantly. Boil and stir 1 minute longer. Remove from heat, stir in walnuts if desired, and pour into buttered 9" square pan. Let stand it room temperature until cool and firm, about 3 hours. Invert pan onto wax paper which has been sprinkled with either powdered sugar or granulated sugar. Cut candy into squares with knife dipped in warm water and roll in sugar.

NOTE: Instead of rolling in sugar, these candies may be dipped in chocolate, if desired.

Honey comes in many flavors

Lemon-Ginger Dressing

Pep up your salads with dressings made with honey. Try this one and experiment with other flavors.

INGREDIENTS:

1/4	cup salad oil
1/4	cup lemon juice
1/2	tsp ground ginger
1/4	tsp salt
1	Tbs honey

METHOD:

Mix all ingredients together well. Chill one hour before using. Shake well before pouring over salad.

Hot Honey-Mustard Dressing

If you like "hot" tasty dressings, try this one. It's good on spinach, or mixed greens.

INGREDIENTS:

1/2	cup honey		1/4	cup vinegar
1	egg		4	Tbs dry mustard
2	Tbs grated horseradish or 3 Tbs prepared horseradish or 2 tsp garlic and 2 tsp chili powder			

METHOD:

Combine all ingredients and cook in double boiler until thick. Cool slightly and pour over greens.

Honey Mustard Dressing

Basic Honey Mustard Dressing can be kept in a tightly sealed jar in the refrigerator for about 6 months, and it can be varied by the addition of herbs. Use for salad dressings, or in sauces served with pork or other meats.

INGREDIENTS:

1	cup Dijon mustard	3	Tbs honey

METHOD:

Blend until thoroughly mixed and creamy. For variety add: 3 Tbs fresh chopped tarragon leaves, or chopped cilantro (especially good with chicken). You can also try adding 1/4 tsp nutmeg or cloves, or 1 tsp ground ginger.

Honey Poppy Seed Dressing

This dressing is delicious with green salads and also with fruit salad.

INGREDIENTS:

3/4	cup mayonnaise
1/3	cup honey
2	Tbs poppy seeds
1	Tbs Dijon mustard
	Salt and pepper to taste

METHOD:

Combine all ingredients; blend well. Makes 1 1/3 cups. Preparation Time: Less than 15 minutes.

Lemon Honey Dressing

If you make enough, you can store in the refrigerator for up to 2 weeks.

INGREDIENTS:

1/4	cup fresh lemon juice
1/3	cup mild honey
1/2	cup salad oil
1/2	tsp salt
	Lemon slice, for garnish

METHOD:

Combine ingredients until blended, Chill. At serving time, float lemon slice in dressing, if desired. Makes about 1 cup. Recipe may be doubled.

Coleslaw Dressing

Coleslaw isn't good unless the dressing is just right. If you like a tarter dressing, add a little bit of vinegar.

INGREDIENTS:

1	Tbs honey
1	Tbs lemon juice
1/2	cup mayonnaise
1/2	tsp celery seed

METHOD:

Combine all ingredients and mix well. Pour over 2 to 4 cups of grated cabbage. Stir and chill. Delicious as dressing on a variety of salads.

Benena's Salad Dressing

Keep this dressing in the refrigerator, ready top go. It's a favorite.

INGREDIENTS:

1	small can tomato sauce
1	cup oil
1/4	cup vinegar
1	Tbs Worchestershire sauce
1	tsp prepared mustard
1	tsp salt
1	cup honey
	dash garlic

METHOD:

With blender or beaters, mix all ingredients. Will keep at least a month in refrigerator. Very good on greens and tomatoes.

Orange Sauce and Glaze

Try this on chicken, turkey or duck.

INGREDIENTS:

1/2   cup fresh orange juice
1-1/2   Tbs salad oil or poultry drippings

1-1/2   Tbs honey

METHOD:

Combine all ingredients well. Use sauce to baste and glaze turkey (or other poultry). Serve remaining sauce with warm turkey. Garnish with halved fresh orange slices.

Lemon Glaze

A variation of the sauce above. This one is especially good on baked chicken breasts.

INGREDIENTS:

2   tsp grated lemon peel, fresh
1/3   cup honey

1/2   cup fresh lemon juice

METHOD:

Combine lemon peel, lemon juice and honey and apply as sauce to turkey, chicken, pork, or meat of your choice when baking or broiling is nearly finished.

INDEX